"Satan's "Evangelistic" Strategy For This New Age

Other Victor Books Titles by Erwin Lutzer

How to Say No to a Stubborn Habit
Managing Your Emotions
When a Good Man Falls
Living with Your Passions
How to Have a Whole Heart in a Broken World

"Satan's *Evangelistic* Strategy For This New Age

Erwin W. Lutzer
& John F. DeVries

VICTOR BOOKS®
A DIVISION OF SCRIPTURE PRESS PUBLICATIONS INC.
USA CANADA ENGLAND

2   3   4   5   6   7   8   9   10   Printing/Year   94   93   92

Unless otherwise indicated, Scripture quotations in this book are from
the *New American Standard Bible,* © the Lockman Foundation 1960,
1962, 1963, 1968, 1971, 1972, 1973, 1975, 1977. The *King James Version*
(KJV) has also been used.

Recommended Dewey Decimal Classification: 133.7
Suggested Subject Headings: NEW AGE MOVEMENT; THE OCCULT

Library of Congress Catalog Card Number: 88-62846
ISBN: 0-89693-633-3

Contents

Why Another Book on the New Age Movement?

*S*ince there already are several fine books available on the New Age Movement, readers may wonder why we thought another one had to be written.

First of all, we found that many of these books analyzed specific aspects of the movement (reincarnation, New Age symbols, or its prophetic significance) without painting the broad picture of how Eastern mysticism is infiltrating all aspects of society. This book gives the overview, the basic presuppositions of New Age thought that crop up in many different forms and guises. Our fervent prayer is that those who read this book will be equipped to identify New Age thought wherever it is found.

Second, this book stresses the disguises of Satan, who is willing to adapt his strategy to suit his audience. Our conviction is that the West is his primary target, and that Eastern religion is being packaged in ways that blend in with the contemporary American-Canadian mindset. The lies of Eden are being sold under labels that appeal to this generation of Westerners. Thus, the notion is propagated that we do not have to give up our Judeo-Christian heritage but merely "move beyond it." This makes the deceit more difficult to detect.

Finally, we did not find a single book that emphasized that the believing church is now standing at the crossroads of an unprecedented opportunity. We acknowledge that Antichrist will eventually rule the world; we know that in the latter days many shall depart from the faith to embrace deception. But we are not prepared to run and hide waiting for the end of the world. Never in our memory have people asked so many excellent questions; never before have people been so hungry for spiritual reality. In becoming open to spiritual pursuits, our generation is also open to pursuing the true bread from heaven who "gives life to the world" (John 6:33).

Some people fall into unbelief by magnifying the power of the devil; others commit the same sin by minimizing the power of God. We intend to avoid both of those errors. Yes, Satan has been given awesome power; yes, we are living in a worldwide spiritual revolution that could culminate in the rule of Antichrist. But God has not left us without resources. Thousands are being converted and others who have been involved in various kinds of occult practices are being delivered from their sins. This message of hope must be fervently told to anyone who will listen.

This book is written to help us understand both the strategy of Satan and the power of our sovereign God. We can assault Satan's kingdom and win battles in the power of the ascended Christ.

Our prayer is that you, the reader, will not only curse the darkness, but light a candle wherever God has planted you.

Erwin W. Lutzer
John F. DeVries

The Development of Satan's Religion of Paganism

Original Lie	Classical Names	Resulting Beliefs	Some Contemporary Expressions
"You will be like God" PRIDE: "I AM GOD"	PANTHEISM	God is a force God is all that exists Matter is illusionary We are all God	Animal rights Environmentalism Human potential Confidence in the deity of man
"You surely shall not die" PRIDE: "I DETERMINE MY OWN DESTINY"	REINCARNATIONISM	Time is cyclical We keep "going around" Evil is explained by karma Evolution	Studies in death/dying Belief there is no judgment Channeling No fear of suicide
"You will know good and evil" PRIDE: "I DETERMINE MY OWN MORALS"	RELATIVISM	There are no absolutes Morality depends on the situation Whatever feels good is right Evil is illusionary	Immorality Rock music Values clarification Confusion because God is both good and evil
"Your eyes will be opened" PRIDE: "I HAVE ALL THE KNOWLEDGE I NEED"	ESOTERICISM	You can achieve enlightenment You can consult inner guides You are the light	Drugs Horoscopes Contact with occult powers TM

Chapter One

The Master Strategist

Many Americans are unaware that this nation has been targeted for a massive takeover. While our military experts are concentrating on bombs and missiles, a different kind of battle is being waged for America's heart and soul. Though we think of it as a battle of ideas, it is actually a battle between two supernatural beings who seek the devotion of men. One is referred to in the Bible as "the god of this world," a malicious and cruel being who seeks to enslave his subjects. The other is the living and true God who delights to set people free from the tyranny of sin and bondage to emotional deprivation.

The eventual outcome of the battle is not in doubt. The god of this world has only as much authority and power as the true God has seen fit to give him. In the end, this wicked spirit will be thrown into the bottomless pit, and be tormented day and night, forever and ever. Satan's days are numbered; his deceptions will come to a bitter end.

Meanwhile, this god whom Christ called "the ruler of this

world," has been granted incredible power to deceive the nations. America, the country that has had the benefit of a Christian consensus, is his primary target. As the influence of biblical Christianity in this country begins to wane, his power is on the increase. A survey of what is taught in schools and what is available on television, in the movies, and in our bookstores proves his strategy is working.

When we use the word *evangelism* we think of winning people to Christ. Indeed, the word *evangel* refers to good news. But there is another form of evangelism, the active recruiting of multitudes for the kingdom of darkness. *Satan is enlisting people to stand with him in his final assault on God.* His message is *presented* as good news, but beneath the appealing jargon is a massive deception. To understand how this is taking place, often under the guise of religion, is the primary reason for this book.

But before we talk strategy, let's just dream for a while.

What if you had a hateful passion to deceive everyone on the face of planet earth? What if you had the ability to inject thoughts into the minds of some people and tempt others to take your suggestions? What if you were preparing for a final worldwide takeover? Suppose you could do all initial planning without being detected. What schemes would you use to get your message across?

More specifically, how would you market your agenda in the United States or Canada?

You would have to sell your product by providing some tangible dividends without arousing unnecessary fear and attention. You'd have to package your ideas in a form that the public would accept. Yet your intentions would have to remain skillfully hidden. Like a fisherman, you'd want to give some immediate gratification and keep the hook out of sight. But we are already too far ahead of the story.

Take a good look at your market.

Here's America. Founded by theists who believed that God exists independently of the world and has given moral laws to His creatures, this nation has been a stronghold for

Christianity. Tens of thousands of missionaries have gone to dozens of countries of the world to share the message of Christ's triumph over sin. Despite high crime and immorality, there is religious freedom and a general respect for the Christian faith.

You've made some inroads by belittling the authority of the Bible. Liberalism, with its belief in the inherent goodness of man coupled with a tolerant, nonjudgmental God, has served you well.

Materialism, the belief that matter alone exists, has given you some delight; belief in the true God has become somewhat obsolete.

The notion that all sexual relationships are legitimate as long as carried on by self-respecting adults has helped destroy the family.

Pornography has contributed to the exploitation of children, the degrading of women, and the widespread rejection that comes through the breakup of families.

There's alcoholism, drugs, and despair.

But there is one thing missing: *you want recognition and worship.*

You also desire personal contact with humans who will interpret their experience as a meeting with the true God whom you hate. In the end you want them to be willing to take your *mark.* You yearn for their loyalty. You want them to worship *you* as God.

So what do you do? You think of as many ways as possible to get people to open their lives to the possibility of the supernatural. You market your ideas by promising to meet needs. You will do for them what God has promised to do for them, but you'll do it more quickly and with less hassle.

So you offer your product and prove it will work:
—without making any moral demands on your clients
—without the confines of just one religion
—without denying them pleasure
—without waiting for God's help
—without them having to humble themselves

So much for our dreaming. With a bit of thought you can see that Satan has many advantages in his quest for the American mind. His "gospel" can be packaged in any deceptive form imaginable. He does not have to be locked into one scheme, one technique, or one all eye-catching commercial.

The Dawn of a New Age

And so before the final age when God wraps up history, we have the worldwide phenomenon called the New Age Movement.

This expression encompasses many different routes to spiritual reality—meditation, crystal healings, out-of-body experiences, hypnosis, and channeling, to name a few. In summary, we can say that New Agers believe that true spirituality can be found in a return to the ancient wisdom of Eastern religions. Hinduism, with its emphasis on a life of quiet contemplation, is inviting to people who are weary of our highly commercialized society. And so the basic doctrines of Eastern thought are becoming standard fare here in the United States.

And what are those Eastern beliefs that lie at the heart of what is called the New Age Movement? God is impersonal—the force, energy, and the one all-pervading reality. In fact, everything is God. Salvation comes by meditation, by an experience that unites us with the divine.

The movement abounds with unrestrained optimism. There is a popular feeling that we are on the verge of a radical breakthrough in the evolutionary process—as great a step as that between the Middle Ages and the Renaissance. The integration of metaphysics, science, and ancient wisdom will succeed where Christianity has failed. The old ways simply will not do for today; we are invited to go to the top of a mountain and look around and view reality from an entirely new perspective.

Whereas Christianity says heaven is in the life to come, the New Age Movement says that heaven can't wait! It is pressing in upon us, simply waiting to be acknowledged and accepted. All around us there are signs that we are entering a new age of peace, where death does not exist and spiritual harmony rules. And we have the potential to make it happen.

How do we claim our spiritual benefits? It's not through the study of doctrine or attending church or even the confession of our sins. We make spiritual contact through one or more techniques that put us in touch with our "true self." One way or another we have to access the basic power of the human mind. By taking a journey within we can find spiritual fulfillment and reality.

The New Age Movement is known by various names. Some of the most common designations are the Age of Aquarius, the New Consciousness, the New Orientalism, Cosmic Humanism, the New World Order, the New Esotericism, and the New Globalism. Whatever the name, the basic presuppositions are the same.

Then there are symbols that represent the movement: the rainbow, pyramids, concentric circles, rays of light, crystals, and the unicorn are the most popular. Often the number 666 is worked into various diagrams and signs. All of these signify that we are saying farewell to the Piscean Age (the era of Christianity) and welcoming the New Age of Aquarius. We are, according to the New Agers, leaving darkness to enter into the era of light.

In the next chapters I shall give seven basic strategies that Satan uses to sell himself to the American public. For now, let's get an overview of what he really wants us to believe. Where did the ideas we generally call the New Age Movement arise? What lies at the root of the present interest in Eastern thought? What is the *content* of Satan's message?

Most of us have heard of the booklet entitled *The Four Spiritual Laws*, written by Bill Bright of Campus Crusade, which summarizes the Good News of the Gospel for the man on the street. In brief, the laws are: (1) God loves you and has a wonderful plan for your life; (2) man is sinful and separated from God; (3) Jesus Christ is God's only provision for man's sin; and (4) we must individually receive Jesus Christ as Saviour and Lord.

Satan has his "gospel" too. Thousands of years ago he gave his basic sales pitch to Adam and Eve in which he set forth four lies which have surfaced in different forms among the major non-Christian religions of the world. We can dub his "gospel" *The Four Spiritual Flaws.*

The Four Spiritual Flaws

The best way for us to understand Satan's gospel of deception is to take a careful look at his first "evangelistic" presentation in the Garden of Eden. There he suggested his own philosophy of life, which Eve accepted with her husband standing by in quiet acquiescence.

Though his methodology changes, the essential content of the message remains the same from generation to generation. In effect, Satan gave Adam and Eve an alternative to obedience to God, spelling out the benefits of such a rebellion.

Eve reminded Satan that God had warned them not to eat of the forbidden tree or they would die. His response was, "You surely shall not die! For God knows that in the day you eat from it your eyes will be opened, and you will be like God, knowing good and evil" (Genesis 3:4-5).

Let's take a closer look at what Satan told our first parents.

1. You will be like God.

Satan promised Adam and Eve that they could set up a rival kingdom; they could be their own God. The teaching is not, "You shall be like gods" (as in the *King James Version* of the Bible), but rather, "You shall be as God" (Elohim).

To be like God is an awesome thought. Man is intelligent enough to know that he is not the creator of the planets, stars, and trees. So this flaw had to be adapted for public consumption. It was easier for man to say, "Yes, I am God, but so is nature—in fact, *everything is God and God is everything.*"

And so *pantheism* came into being to make Satan's lie more believable. This view of God which lies at the heart of the New Age Movement is the foundation of ancient Hinduism: the universe is fundamentally a spiritual reality because everything that exists is God. It follows that matter is an illusion; through meditation we can be released from the influence of the material world and become one with God. We really already are God, but in a sense we are still becoming God too!

Just glance through a typical New Age journal and you will see that the movement is profoundly spiritual. Here are a few samples of the seminars you will see offered: *Trance States and Healing, Being More Than Psychic, Miracles and Other Realities, Hypnosis and Sleep Programming,* and the list goes on. We are told to move away from religion toward true spirituality.

For the New Age Movement, God is an impersonal energy force that we can plug into if we have the right mindset. In the process we come to realize our basic unity with the whole universe; then we are prepared to accept our own divinity. As Shirley MacLaine put it, "We already know everything. The knowingness of our own divinity is the highest intelligence."

The implications of this view will be explained later. For now it is sufficient to remember that the idea of man's deity originated through the words of a snake who "channeled" Satan in Eden. This lie is widely believed.

2. You surely shall not die.

This was a second fabrication used by Satan to minimize the consequences of disobedience. Death is the one event we all fear most. Even atheists have been known to dread the final step into the unknown.

This myth must also be adapted for wholesale distribution. The fact is that people do die; a trip to the local cemetery is a convincing argument for the universality of this experience. How then can this lie be believed by the general population?

The answer is found in the doctrine of reincarnation. Yes, your body (which pantheism believes is illusionary anyway) may die. But *you* go on living in another body. You go round and round, getting as many chances at perfection as you need. Death is not to be feared because it changes nothing essential in one's personality. You take with you the wisdom accumulated in this life and use it in the next. This experience is to be accepted as the natural consequence of cyclical time. There is no personal God to whom you must give account. The laws of *karma* (to be discussed later) move relentlessly onward. Thus the fear of death can be confidently removed from man's mind and imagination. In fact, death is welcomed. A New Age couple who kissed each other before they jumped off the Golden Gate Bridge in San Francisco left a note in the car in which the man wrote, "I love you all; wish I could stay, but I must hurry. The suspense is killing me."

In our chapter on reincarnation we will show its astounding implications for understanding suffering and morality. In fact, as reincarnationism gains popularity in America, we can almost predict what this will mean for our culture and values. More of that later.

3. You will know good and evil.

"Indeed, has God said?" Satan began (Genesis 3:1). He got Eve to doubt whether a good God would actually restrict her and her husband from something as good as a beautiful tree. If they ate of the tree, he went on to say, they would be able to make their own decisions regarding morality. They, of themselves, would have secret knowledge about good and evil. The decision to take Satan's suggestion led to relativism in morality.

While watching an interview on television, I heard a woman admit to having an affair with another woman's husband. Sensing that this still may be considered improper by some of her listening audience, she felt constrained to add, "Of course, what I am doing may not be right for everyone, but it's what is best for me."

This is what is known as relativism—what is good for me is not necessarily what is good for you. Nothing is intrinsically right or wrong; the situation determines morality. No need to consult God about moral choices. You can do whatever seems good, depending on the circumstances.

Though such a view might sound rather harmless, it has far-reaching implications for governments as well as marriages. Indeed, as will be shown later, relativism leads to unrelenting cruelty and mindless despair.

Morality poses an especially formidable problem for what is known as the New Age Movement. After all, if all is God and God is all, then *evil must be God too!* Distinctions between right and wrong end up being illusionary.

Satan's strategy is to dupe the world into believing that it can make its own decisions about right and wrong. A teenager gave himself to the devil and later, in an effort to break all 10 of the commandments, killed his mother and two siblings. He commented, "Satanism has made me a better person." The implications of this deception are explained in chapter 6.

Mankind has paid an incredible price for believing this lie of Eden.

4. Your eyes will be opened.

At the beginning of the conversation in Eden, Satan undermined Eve's faith in what God had said. Now that an objective source of truth was nicely set aside, what would serve as a substitute? The answer was Eve's sensual desires. The text reads, "When the woman saw that the tree was good for food, and that it was a delight to the eyes, and that the tree was desirable to make one wise, she took from its fruit and ate; and she gave also to her husband with her, and he ate" (Genesis 3:6).

When Eve saw that the tree was pleasant to the eyes, she disregarded God's command and ate the fruit. Satan had promised that her eyes would be opened; her disobedience would lead to an experience of enlightenment. Her motto was, "If it feels good, do it!"

This philosophy, known as esotericism, lies at the heart of the New Age Movement. We are told that there is a "transformation of consciousness" that initiates us into true spirituality. Historically, the esoterics believed they were privy to special knowledge that was hidden from the masses. We must leave religion behind and venture into new dimensions of knowledge and enlightenment. The eventual goal is spiritual conversion.

Those who promote the New Age Movement believe that there can be no universal theology (the religions of the world have contradictions that cannot be resolved); therefore doctrine is not important. What *is* important is a religious experience, the feeling of oneness with the force, the energy called God. Reason doesn't help you. You must use the right technique to get plugged into ultimate reality. Irrationality is in; reason is out. The basic lie is: *feel, don't think!*

Like the other lies of Eden, this one has some interesting implications. Logically, it leads not only to absurdities, but to the destruction of any objective truth.

Let's review the four lies:

1. You will be like God (Pantheism).
2. You surely shall not die (Reincarnationism).
3. You will know good and evil (Relativism).
4. Your eyes will be opened (Esotericism).

Taken together, these four lies have the power to mislead multitudes in this life and to bring damnation in the life to come. Whatever we may say of the New Age Movement, it is certainly not new. Its basic beliefs were enunciated in Eden and have been a part of ancient paganism since the beginning of human existence.

What is the bottom line in these four spiritual flaws? It is *the self-sufficiency of mankind*, the belief that the source of all reality exists in the human mind. When we take a journey within, we find that we are God; through channeling we can contact masters who have preceded us. We can be the source of our own morality and discover the right technique to be spiritually fulfilled. On our own we can become all that we can be.

We are told that man's problem is not sin but ignorance. Through enlightenment, we can solve all of our problems and bring about a spiritual transformation that will bring peace and brotherhood to this world. All this comes by our own initiative and strength.

The New Age Movement derives much of its inspiration from Eastern religions, but in this country it is packaged for American audiences. On this side of the ocean, its mood is upbeat, faddish, and success-oriented. It's a strange mixture of Hinduism, pagan magic, and mainstream American values—good health, wealth, and individualism.

It's selling well.

A Cultural Shift

Marilyn Ferguson in her popular book *The Aquarian Conspiracy* introduces us to the basic beliefs and strategies of the New Age Movement. She writes that an "irrevocable shift" is overtaking us. It is not a new system, but a new *mind*. There is an underground movement that is changing society based on an "enlarged concept of human potential . . . a transformation of personal consciousness."[1] She predicts we are at a breakthrough in the next step of human evolution.

Yes, there is a change occurring. Military strategists shift the focus of a war to deceive the enemy or to achieve more daring objectives. Satan's strategy is to move beyond the mindset of the past few decades to boldly capture the allegiance of the present generation. Though in the past he operated largely undetected, today he is making visible overtures to people who are seeking spiritual reality.

We often think of America as inundated with secularism, the belief that God is irrelevant to human life and existence. Philosophers spread the word that man has to create his own reason to exist; he cannot look to any spiritual powers for answers to ultimate questions. Scientists, in tune with this perspective, teach that man evolved through the animal world; therefore humans are simply the product of impersonal forces such as time and chance. Though only a very few Americans claim to be atheists, millions live as if they are; that is, they believe God is totally unrelated to the 20th century. The bottom line is that man is totally alone in the world and therefore *there is no supernatural dimension to the universe.*

If that's your picture of America, it needs revision. A recent survey conducted by the well-known Jesuit priest Dr. Andrew Greeley of the University of Chicago showed that 67 percent of Americans now confess to believe in the supernatural; 29 percent believe in reincarnation and 42 percent believe they have been in contact with someone who has died.[2] The word is out that there is a supernatural world waiting to be explored complete with psychic and ascended masters. What is more, this world cannot be enjoyed by looking outside of ourselves. We can only find this hidden dimension by taking a journey within, by exploring the potential of our own minds. Adventure is as close as a self-help seminar.

It is not an exaggeration to say that these ideas are becoming the controlling realities of our time. Turn on the TV, look at the magazines in your local grocery store, or listen to your friends talk about their latest adventure and you will discover that we are in the middle of a massive spiritual revolution. There's little doubt that Americans have found a new world of reality that a previous generation did not know existed. It's a world of miracles, out-of-body experiences, and conversations with entities that claim to have lived thousands of years ago. *America is being converted to a new religion.*

Is this just a fad? Or is this nation becoming absorbed into a grand plan, masterminded by Satan who hungers for recognition and worship? Could he be getting the world conditioned to accept miracles so that it will be ready to accept the coming great counterfeit miracle-worker?

Where New Meets Old

Read the Old Testament and you will be impressed with the number of times the name *Babylon* appears. The city began when men rebelled against God and attempted to build a tower—called Babel in Genesis 11:9—that would reach to the heavens. From those occult beginnings, Babylon eventually rose to become a dominant power with its sorcery permeating the ancient world. The prophets of God condemned it because it represented all that was most evil in man's attempts to dethrone God.

What did the Babylonians believe that was so perverse? Isaiah 47:8-11 summarizes their religion:

> Now, then, hear this, you sensual one, who dwells securely, who says in your heart, "I am, and there is no one besides me. I shall not sit as a widow, nor shall I know the loss of children."
>
> But these two things shall come upon you suddenly in one day: loss of children and widowhood. They shall come on you in full measure in spite of your many sorceries, in spite of the great power of your spells. And you felt secure in your wickedness and said, "No one sees me."
>
> Your wisdom and your knowledge, they have deluded you; for you have said in your heart, "I am, and there is no one besides me."
>
> But evil will come on you which you will not know how to charm away; and disaster will fall on you for which you cannot atone, and destruction about which you do not know will come on you suddenly.

Take a close look at the text. Ancient Babylon had a spiritual religion built upon blasphemous premises:

1. The deity of man—"I am, and there is no one besides me."
2. A false belief in triumph over death—"I shall not sit as a widow, nor shall I know the loss of children."
3. Moral relativism—"Hear this, you sensual one."
4. Esotericism, or private enlightenment through mystical spiritual experiences—"Your many sorceries . . . the great power of your spells."

Texe Marrs in his book *Dark Secrets of the New Age* lists nearly 30 rituals and beliefs found in ancient Babylon that are practiced today in the New Age Movement! Everything from reincarnation to occult meditation was commonplace 3,000 years ago.[3]

The New Testament predicts that at the end of this age the religion of ancient Babylon will again stand in opposition to God. A woman clothed in purple and scarlet is described by the Apostle John as having the mystery name on her forehead, "BABYLON THE GREAT, THE MOTHER OF HARLOTS AND OF THE ABOMINATIONS OF THE EARTH" (Revelation 17:5).

We may not be certain that the New Age Movement of today is indeed the final Babylon of Revelation. What we do know is that *the final Babylon will practice the same occult religion as that of ancient Babylon.* That is the religion which is now sweeping the Western world and gaining widespread acceptance among all levels of our society.

The *New* Age thus is a revival of the *Old* Age. And the New Age may well turn out to be the *Final* Age. For as modern Babylon gains in momentum, it will once again assault the heavens and shake its fist in the face of God. Satan's plan is to initiate as many people as he can so they will stand with him in his *religious* opposition to God. How good will Satan's counterfeit be? The Apostle John writes, "And they worshipped the beast, saying, 'Who is like the beast, and who is able to wage war with him?'" (Revelation 13:4)

What are the techniques being used to promote Satan's myths? Who are his most popular "evangelists"? What are the implications of their teaching? How far have these ideas infiltrated our homes and schools? And finally, what can we do to dispel these false beliefs? These are some of the questions we hope to answer in the pages that follow.

If you are looking for another pessimistic analysis of our present condition, you may be surprised. The bad news is that Satan is winning the allegiance of millions in his clever campaign to take over the world. But, as we shall see, along with this has come a marvelous and unmatched opportunity to share the true Gospel. Never in our history have people so enthusiastically sought to fill the void in their lives; never before have they been so willing to talk about Christ.

This is the day for the believing church to take its message to a waiting world. The New Age Movement has rushed in to fill the vacuum left by a timid and sometimes fearful church. May God keep us from the unbelief that would concede this world to Satan!

It's a day for discernment; it's also a day for opportunity.

Chapter Two

Capturing
the American Mind

*A*con artist in Chicago had a successful scheme that worked like this: he would contact a prospective client, assuring the man that a few hundred dollars invested in a specified business venture would double in a matter of months.

The client was leery, but the sales pitch was so impressive that he decided to try it. A few hundred dollars was not much to lose.

A few months later, the con man made good his promise; he returned to bring the man double his money. His extravagant claims appeared to be true.

A month later the con man returned to his client with a similar promise. This time the investment was a few thousand dollars. Once again the investor returned an impressive dividend.

So it went. Each time the client developed more confidence in his broker; each time the amount of money increased.

Finally the happy client was willing to give his friend $50,000 with the promise of still higher profits. With that, the broker disappeared.

Scam operators will tell you to follow some basic nonnegotiable rules if you want to deceive the public:

1. Never lose sight of your long-term goal—the enslavement of your prospects. Be temporarily satisfied with an inch if it can become the basis for a yard later on.

2. Your clients must develop confidence in you. Do nothing to arouse suspicion or fear.

3. Use bait that will appeal to the customer and at the same time keep the "hook" skillfully hidden.

4. Make promises that show the personal benefits of your product. Keep as many promises as possible.

5. Have as many lures as there are tastes among the masses. There is no limit to the numbers of doors that can lead to the final goal of control and entrapment.

Let's review Satan's strategy: we've learned that he has a master plan to deceive the nations of the world. To do this he must first redefine mankind's definition of God. Rather than thinking of God as the personal Creator, Satan would like man to think of God as everything that exists. Then man can think of himself as God too.

Second, Satan wants to redefine death so that people think of it as a pleasant transition without any accountability to a personal God. You just go around as many times as you need to, and eventually you will get to nirvana.

Third, he wants us to come to our own definition of what is good or evil. Moral relativism serves his purpose because it breaks down the fiber of a nation and leads to personal emotional entrapment.

Fourth, he promotes esotericism, the belief that reality can be reduced to a personal experience of enlightenment. Man can feel initiated as an enlightened one if he has the right mystical encounter.

Why all this effort? Satan hates God and therefore hates God's people. He desires the allegiance of all the people of the world. And the only way he can have that kind of commitment is to disguise himself, appear as a helper of mankind, and, if possible, develop a point of contact between himself and people. As Billy Graham has said, Satan is not about to begin a church for the masses called the First Church of Satan.

In fact, as we shall see, his ultimate strategy is to aggravate the problems of society and then prescribe a solution for the damage he has created! To gain greater foothold in individual lives, *he develops programs to recruit people into spiritual slavery.* In the end, he wants man to join him in his final battle against God. Meanwhile, like a con artist, he keeps as many promises as possible with the final price tag hidden.

The Satanic Advantage

Truth, despite all of its awesome power for good, has one glaring disadvantage. Truth always has a narrow focus because *there is usually only one right answer to most questions.* Two plus two equals four. Only one number satisfies the equation. But false answers are endless. Indeed, there is almost an infinite number of wrong answers to the simplest mathematical question.

The same principle holds for spiritual truth and error. Consider the claim of Christ: "I am the way, and the truth, and the life; no one comes to the Father, but through Me" (John 14:6). Christ taught that there was but one way to God. But that means that there are numerous false ways that may be used to attempt to reach the true God.

To put it simply: there is only one way to be right, but many ways to be wrong. Therefore, *Satan can have as many ways to deceive the United States as there are interests among Americans.* Whatever appeals to human beings can become a lure to the ultimate goal of self-worship and spiritual bondage. Satan can use religion, health fads, pseudoscience, and a host of other covers to plant seeds that will eventually bear bitter fruit.

Since there is an endless number of ways to be deceived, you can enter the occult stream at any point and eventually arrive at the same destination as your friends who stepped in at a different point along the shoreline.

What requirement is necessary for a technique or practice to lead to the darker side of the spirit world? Just one: it must in some way violate the first commandment, "You shall have no other gods before Me" (Exodus 20:3).

Any object that purports to give *supernatural* guidance violates this commandment, for the Scriptures teach that we should look to the true God alone for direction in our lives. Ouija boards, horoscopes, fortune-tellers, and dozens of other such practices violate this basic principle. These practices are a substitute for faith in the living God.

Back in May 1988 headlines around the world beamed the news that Nancy Reagan, wife of the President, frequently received counsel from an astrologer to make important political decisions. *Time* magazine reported, "In Reagan's mind, an actor's superstitions coexist unabashedly alongside a deep, if unstructured, Christian faith. He is untroubled by the contradictions between the paranormal phenomena that intrigue him and strict church doctrine, which rejects such divinations as the tools of the devil."[1]

Perhaps the former President had never read Isaiah 47:13-14, where God angrily taunts the Babylonians for their reliance on astrology:

> You are wearied with your many counsels; let now the astrologers, those who prophesy by the stars, those who predict by the new moons, stand up and save you from what will come upon you. Behold, they have become like stubble, fire burns them; they cannot deliver themselves from the power of the flame; there will be no coal to warm by, nor fire to sit before!

In other Old Testament passages, astrology is referred to as an abomination because it bypasses God in the search for wisdom. It is not too strong to say that those who participate in it are unwittingly shaking their fists in His face. Interestingly, when the pagans became Christians in Ephesus they brought all of their occult books and burned them in the fire (Acts 19:19).

Second, any practice or object that claims *supernatural* power to heal (either physically or emotionally) also takes the place of faith in the one true God. Crystals, acupuncture, and numerous psychic therapies that use "healing guides" make such claims. Sometimes healings do occur, but these miracles occur under the power of Satan.

Medical science does not fall under this judgment because it works through natural means to effect a cure. As we shall see later, the New Age Movement wants us to extend the boundaries of nature to include psychic phenomena and spiritual powers.

Third, any practices which purport to receive *supernatural* information from the dead violate the first commandment. God has given us His word so that we might have sufficient knowledge about spiritual realities. Thus all witchcraft, seances, and channeling come under the direct condemnation of God. They are rebellion and idolatry.

Principles of Salesmanship

As we've noted earlier, the Eastern religions best represent the lies of Eden. But to expect Americans to become Hindus is both impossible and unneccessary. Impossible, because we are too materialistic to leave the pursuit of money and opt for a life of perpetual meditation. Unnecessary, because there are other equally valid ways to ensnare the unwary. Just as you use meat to trap a bear, a worm to catch a fish, and seed to lure a bird, so you adapt your strategy for your market. Whatever Americans like, they can have—almost. They can keep their money, pursue their pleasures, and satisfy their egos. All that they have to do is broaden their faith so that it reaches beyond the one true God and His Son, Jesus Christ.

Eastern religion therefore seeps into the West appropriately wrapped. This religion, as someone has said, "is one that allows us to keep our BMWs and the designer tennis outfits, but allows us to achieve enlightenment anyway . . . it's a new age of Aquarius that accepts MasterCard and Dolby stereos."[2] In other words, the lies of Eden appear as friendly faces.

Let's look at this strange blend of East and West more carefully, examining the principles used to sell the lies.

1. Promise that your techniques bring success.

Americans are pragmatic. Success, financial and otherwise, is highly prized. Thus New Age thought, if it is to be widely accepted, must fit in with the success syndrome.

Napoleon Hill's book *Think and Grow Rich* has sold millions of copies and is highly recommended as a textbook for those who seek to change themselves through the power of positive thinking and self-motivation. The book turns on this basic premise: *anything the human mind can believe, the human mind can achieve.*

This revelation of the awesome powers of the human mind was communicated to Hill by disembodied spirits. In an earlier work, *Grow Rich with Peace of Mind*, he says he has evidence that unseen friends hover above him; he calls them The School of the Masters who can travel anywhere they choose. One of these masters came to his study to reveal this supreme secret and then told Hill to reveal this "truth" to the world.[3]

Christians know that these disembodied masters are actually demonic spirits who communicated with Hill to give him this special revelation. Clearly, the message was demonic: it is simply not true that we can achieve whatever we believe. This revelation is basic Hinduism crafted for the American mind. The Eastern religions believe that the mind (or realm of the spirit) is the only reality, and that the mind has the power to create whatever it desires. If indeed we could achieve whatever we believe, we would be God— which is of course exactly what the New Age teaches.

Here you have Hinduism American-style. The basic lie that man is God has been cleverly designed for the benefit of American business. And, because Satan wants to keep as many promises as possible, it works. Ask those who have benefited from Napoleon Hill's book.

In countless ways American businessmen are imbibing Eastern deceptions about the power of the mind. But they are doing it to increase sales and productivity. Pacific Bell, Proctor and Gamble, TRW, Ford, and Polaroid are only a few of the dozens of companies that now either have hired gurus or are teaching seminars based on New Age thought. The November 23, 1987 issue of *Fortune* magazine says, "The gurus have adapted their standard programs to suit business clients and are finding a fast growing market among corporations still searching for *the* answer to productivity problems."[4] These power-of-the-mind teachers include *Forum* (formerly *est*, short for Erhard Seminar Training), Scientology, and a rash of other human potential groups.

Is this just group dynamics? The author of the *Fortune* article says that some of these groups use psychological techniques "that can induce ordinary people to suspend their judgment, surrender themselves to their instructors, and even adopt new fundamental beliefs."[5] Their aim, he says, is "to alter people—or corporations—radically by unleashing energies that purportedly remain unused in most of us. They seek to liberate the mind, they say, by 'breaking chains of habit and passivity.' "[6]

Does it work? Opinions are divided. Although some companies prove it does by pointing to their profit columns, others say it isn't worth it because of what it does to the participants. Carl Raschke of the University of Denver is quoted as saying, "It puts people in a more mellow mood and makes them more compliant . . . but it certainly does not make them more productive. It robotizes them."[7] Some people forced to participate in such mind-expanding experiences have sued for psychological damage.

Supporters of these human potential seminars are convinced that they have found the secret that can solve the problems of business stagnation. Thus the basic occult dictum that you have all the resources you need within you is finding its way into more and more of the corporate world. This is a new form of spirituality that considers indulgence to be a virtue.

Of course, there is a legitimate use of the power of positive thinking. Someone has pointed out that the little engine that said, "I think I can! I think I can!" was much more likely to make it up the hill than a pessimistic engine. But if the railway tracks were washed out on the top of the hill, positive thinking would not have helped. Similarly, no one has the ability to actually "reorder reality" just by using the mind.

In the future we can expect more attempts to blend Eastern thought with American business procedures. We will hear that the mind has unlimited potential, and contact will be made with "higher invisible forces."

2. Mix truth and error.

Americans are interested in their health. Here again they differ from the Easterners for whom longevity is not a high priority. If Satan wants to reach those Americans who have no interest in mind-expanding seminars but who are into health food, he will have to design a special program just for them. Remember, there are as many routes to the occult as there are interests among Americans.

Here is where some truth enters. Americans know that they have bad eating habits: too much cholesterol, too little protein, and too little exercise. There are good reasons to change diets and to eat natural foods. There is a desperate need for more physical activity and vitamins. So far, so good.

What happens is subtle and enlightening. Millions of Americans are now combining proper eating habits with psychic or spiritual experiences to create a "holistic approach" to health. This new fad tries to combine the mind sciences with physical science to achieve a sense of well-being. Thus ingredients derived from Eastern philosophies are deftly mixed with legitimate dietary concerns. Without knowing it, many are introduced to the New Age agenda.

An advertisement for a Natural Health convention to be held in Chicago offers seminars on the need to return to herbs rather than drugs and natural diets. There are also lectures on reflexology, proper visualization, and how to revitalize your electrical body. One lecture is entitled *Biolectrical Treatment for Cancer, Lupus, and MS.* The convention stresses the principles of "free thinking" and "nutritional therapy." The science of the mind is just as important as the science of the body. For healing, we must have a model that is based on energy, not matter.

Read a few more of the seminar titles: *Awakening the Healer Within—A Practitioner's Introduction to Therapeutic Touch* or *Psychoimmunity and the Healing Process*, which promises that we can unite our mind and body and "we will access our own innate abilities to achieve health and balance in our lives."

Even AIDS is curable, the ads assure us. With the proper alignment of mind, body, and spirit we can tap those latent resources to fight disease. One ad says that the leader of the seminar "knows in his heart that AIDS can be healed" because "we can transcend our dis-ease states." Add acupuncture, self-hypnosis, and biofeedback and you can achieve "holistic healing."

Other seminars introduce Eastern philosophy with fewer subtleties. Yoga is a guide to health; transcendental meditation leads to better circulation and more restful sleep.

Who would not want both wealth and health? Both can be ours through understanding the latent power of the mind. Understandably, the New Age promises are attractive to millions of Americans.

There is, of course, truth to the idea that the mind influences the body. Doctors tell us that the rate of recovery from surgery often depends on the attitude of the patient.

Those who are optimistic about their recovery have a better chance than the pessimists who expect to die. Laughter, it is said, releases natural forces that fight disease and promote health. The body and the mind are delicately balanced, each affecting the other.

Where then is the error? The health fads referred to here ascribe to the mind greater powers—supernatural powers—than it actually has. The premise is that the mind actually has complete control over the body—or at least it *can* have, if you combine a right diet with the right mental framework. The assumption is that *you can be your own healer because you are your own god.* One devotee claims that "unseen doctors are working through me."

The witch doctor is back, but this time he holds high-priced seminars and has a scientific explanation for his occult powers.

Eastern religions are adapted for Americans in other ways. The Hindus do not eat cows because the sacred animals are divine. And, with their belief in reincarnation, there is also the possibility that one would be eating an animal who had actually been a human being in a previous life. When Eastern vegetarianism is promoted in the West, it is done for other reasons, such as "meat makes one violent . . . a vegetarian diet makes one at peace with oneself." Commenting on this change of rationale, Robert A. Morey writes, "The Eastern concept that one could be eating his dear grandmother at McDonald's would not win many converts in the Western world. Thus Eastern ascetic vegetarianism has been redesigned for the Western palate and lightly seasoned with religious and psychological terminology."[8]

Millions of Americans are thus being introduced to the Eastern science of mind through the Western science of nutrition. By combining the two under the banner of a "holistic approach to health," people are swept up in the basic lie about their own role in health and achievement. Even if the basic mixture is 20 percent lies and 80 percent truth, Satan has made progress. With a foot in the door, he presses on for greater conquests. As Enoch Burr observed, "In the hands of unbelief, half truths are made to do the work of whole falsehoods."

3. Sell your product under the guise of science.

For the most part, Americans stand transfixed under the god called science. In any discussion the sentence that begins, "Scientists say . . . " ends all argument. To disagree with the conclusion of science is to display naiveté and, worse, stupidity. There are millions out there who say that they will not accept anything unless it is scientific.

For them, the master strategist has just the right sales approach. Occult practices are advertised as "scientific." Combining ancient wisdom with modern science packs a powerful punch. In fact, the impression is sometimes given that modern science is finally catching up to the grand ancient wisdom of the East!

Thousands respond to ads like this:

**INTRODUCTORY OFFER . . . ASTROFLASH
LET THE COMPUTERS AND THE STARS WORK FOR YOU.
MORE THAN A HOROSCOPE . . . A COMPLETE
ASTROLOGICAL STUDY
DEVELOPED BY WORLD FAMOUS ASTROLOGER . . .
GET THIS $100.00 VALUE FOR ONLY $19.95.**

All you must do is provide your date, time, and place of birth along with the money. The guarantee is that "perhaps you will learn for the first time what makes you so individual a personality . . . and what your immediate future holds."

Talk about strategy! This ad guarantees: (1) personal attention, (2) the combination of ancient wisdom and modern technology, and (3) the promise of a six-month forecast. And, very probably, *it works.* Many say that such predictions have uncanny accuracy. And once you have proven the value of such an investment, you will develop a dependency that leads to enslavement. Having broken the first commandment by turning away from God to the guidance of the stars, you have entered the world of the occult.

Then there are crystals, those beautiful stones that diffuse sunlight, showing bright and changing colors. The ancient Greeks called them "frozen light" and the Romans believed these stones had magical powers. In Japanese legend, small crystals represented the breath of the White Dragon. Today they are associated with magical powers for physical and spiritual health.

But Americans are not into magic—it is simply too unscientific. If crystals are going to be introduced in our society they must come wrapped in the tissue of scientific research. So various "natural" or "scientific" explanations for the power of crystals abound.

One book says that crystals emit subatomic particles that affect the energy vibrations of the body. Thus crystals can help your body become better "aligned" with itself and induce physical healing. Seminars are available on how to choose the crystal that is right for you.

Another expert explained that crystals have power to be programmed like a computer chip through the power of our own concentration. They can also magnify our moods. If we are depressed, they will respond to our depression; if we are joyful, they will magnify our joy. And if we are living with self-incrimination (guilt), there are crystals that can take that away too.

Do crystals work? Like other relics, beads, and occult objects, those who put faith in crystals get results. *Time* magazine quotes one woman as saying that she was healed from a fungus and stomach trouble by the subtle energy of crystals.[9] Hundreds of others give similar testimonials. *Satan makes these objects work.*

Magic is out; pseudoscience is in. As long as there is an "explanation," many assume it must be so—especially if some people say it "worked" for them.

On August 16, 1987 a "harmonic convergence" occurred in different places around the world. New Age disciples held hands and hummed, hoping to pick up vibrations of energy or the force. This was to promote love among humanity but also to "plug into" the energy available for individual needs.

The organizers of this event said that we should come together to "promote an energy field of trust, harmony, and love on earth." By surrendering to spirit-led direction within and to the universal power of God, other "spirit-beings" would know of our intentions. These "spirit-beings" are "light-beings" from the heavens that have been attracted to the earth to observe our choices and to help shift us to love and peace.

Why August 16, 1987? The ancients prophesied of powerful days in which to invoke harmony and love. The explanation is that there was a convergence of the planets on August 16, causing a major shift in "energy cycles" on the earth. Although astronomers denied that there was any such convergence of the planets, the widespread belief was that there was a scientific explanation as to how humans could plug into this transfer of energy. Hundreds of thousands believed it.

Did it work? In Chicago, where hundreds gathered on the shores of Lake Michigan, many claim to have experienced a surge of energy and even spoke of encounters with supernatural beings. Later one man remarked to another, "I was healed . . . thank you, whoever you are." No doubt the god of this world had sent his emissaries (the beings of light called demons) to perform some miracles.

The real "harmonic convergence" on August 16, 1987 was the coming together of the occult and pseudoscience to form an alliance that was believable for thousands of people. People who disdain magic accept it when it is explained as an "energy field" or the "alignment of planets."

Scientific explanations are also given for dozens of other New Age techniques such as acupuncture, hypnotism, and out-of-body experiences. *The boundaries of science must be extended to include the work of Satan if Americans are to accept his power.* Thus science ventures out further and further into the paranormal or spiritual realm.

4. Use language to disguise your identity.

Language is our most precise and powerful medium. Men can be distinguished from animals simply on the basis of speech. Though animals can communicate with one another, they are not capable of abstract thought and the formation of sentences. The power of speech, strictly speaking, belongs only to man.

The word *occult* means "hidden" or "secret." For this reason it is always associated with deception. The devil is a master of disguise. He cannot speak plainly, but must always protect his true identity with the cloak of misinformation. The flexibility of language serves him well. It is easier to create a new vocabulary than to speak in descriptive terms that people understand.

Suppose insurance executives were expected to attend a seminar entitled *How to Become a Hindu.* Around the table stand a half-dozen Indian masters in native dress. Needless to say, the seminar would not be well attended. The executives would be much more receptive if the leader wore a three-piece suit with a copy of the *Wall Street Journal* under his arm and the seminar was called *How Meditation Can Help You Increase Sales.* The teaching would be essentially the same, but communication takes place best within a cultural framework.

We've learned that Satan adapts his sales strategy to suit the culture and interests of Americans. Therefore, the use of the right terms is essential in getting his message across.

A book that has been on the best-seller list for months is entitled *Communion* by Whitley Strieber, a man who has had a long-standing interest in the occult. In it he relates the chilling story of how he was abducted by strange beings who appeared to him, had sex with him, and tortured him. Clearly this was a demonic invasion; he was even able to identify the pagan gods (demons) who had visited him. The book is frightening, for it has the earmarks of truth. Indeed, when Strieber awoke from the experience, he had two triangles inscribed on his left forearm. Strieber tells us that his wife received a special revelation as to what the book's title should be:

> One night in April (my wife) talked in her sleep. . . . Suddenly she said in a strange basso profundo voice: "The book must not frighten people. You should call it *Communion* because that's what it's about."[10]

Yes, it is about communion, but not the kind we generally enjoy with one another and with God. This is communion with evil spirits who delight in duplicating religious experiences. Notice the reason for the title: *it must not frighten people.* Satan slants meanings and words to his own advantage. He does not obey the "truth in packaging" laws.

Maharishi, a spokesman for transcendental meditation, candidly talked about how TM should be marketed in America.

> Whenever . . . religion dominates the mass consciousness, transcendental deep meditation should be taught in terms of religion. . . . Today when politics is guiding the destiny of man, the teaching would be primarily based on the field of politics and secondarily on the plane of economics. . . . It seems, for the present, that this transcendental deep meditation should be made available to people through the agencies of government.[11]

His point is clear: transcendental meditation is a religion, but it can be presented in other ways, depending on the dominant worldview of society. If people are interested in health, it can be sold as a technique to lower blood pressure or control stress. This was the basis upon which it was taught in American schools funded by our tax dollars. Thus, though Christianity cannot be taught in our classrooms, Hinduism can be.

In *New Thought* magazine, an article stated that we can prove that we are spiritual beings, creatures of light and cosmic substance. This information, the author went on to say, should be taught from kindergarten upward. Then followed these words, "But unless we name it something else—like bioenergetic physics—it's going to remain a religious idea and subsequently stay out of our schools.... This is not religion. This is science."[12]

If it can be sold as politics, sell it as such; if it can be sold as religion, do it; better yet, sell it as science. Use whatever label that seems convenient for this generation.

Shirley MacLaine's drama based on her book *Out On a Limb* was aired on national TV as a seven-hour miniseries. To my knowledge, few protested this successful campaign to sell Hinduism to the American public. It was done under the guise of a personal documentary, exploring new forms of thought. Imagine the uproar if someone would have attempted to film his testimony of faith in Christ. Promoting religion has no place on prime-time TV, critics would argue.

Verbal deceptions abound. The common person, even if irreligious, still has a healthy fear of mediums. So the New Agers have dropped the term and use "channeler" instead. Instead of talking to demons, they speak to "entities," "inner guides," or even "ascended masters." That sounds harmless—appealing in fact.

How can people accept such clever distortions? Paul, in the New Testament, answered that question: "But evil men and impostors will proceed from bad to worse, deceiving and being deceived" (2 Timothy 3:13).

Remember Satan's strategy of twisted language: *tell them what they want to hear, but give them what you want them to have.*

5. Communicate through entertainment.

Read these words carefully: "For my ally is the Force and a powerful ally it is. . . . Its energy surrounds us and binds us. . . . Luminous beings we are. Not this crude matter. You must feel the Force around you. Here between you and me . . . between the rock. Everywhere . . . even in the land."

Who said those words? A Hindu guru? He might have, for this fits perfectly with the Eastern notion of spirit beings, with God as "the force." But it was said by Yoda of *Star Wars* fame. Millions of children (and adults) were absorbed in a fantasy that had a religious message.

In chapter 9 we shall look more closely at how New Age ideas have infiltrated our homes. But all you have to do is page through the movie ads in your newspaper. The titles tell the story—occult themes are everywhere. Either overtly or subtly the message preached in the Garden of Eden is repeated for millions. The content has not changed, just the "medium" has.

The master strategist has all but captured the entertainment industry of the United States. The message is clear: *you can have fun while you learn to change your perception of reality.*

6. Stress techniques that glorify self-effort rather than rational religious principles or doctrine.

We've already learned that the New Age Movement stresses techniques, points of contacts between individuals, and self-discovery. Doctrine, especially religious convictions, are despised. Belief in objective truth gets in the way of experiencing mystical oneness with the cosmos. Nobody ever had a transformation of consciousness because he learned religious doctrine. Particularly disdainful is any doctrine of sin, for that contradicts the belief in boundless human potential.

The difficulty Satan has in the United States is that we have had a Christian heritage, a residue of which is still left on our culture. Since this stands in the way of accepting

Eastern thought, there is only one way to overcome this hurdle: it is to say that one can still be a Christian *and* accept New Age thought too.

To pull this off, Satan must get Americans to alter their understanding of truth. No longer can we think in terms of right or wrong. *Truth must be redefined so as to encompass even contradictory or absurd ideas.* Christianity can be true, but so can Hinduism and Buddhism. You can be right though your view contradicts mine, and I'm still right too. Strictly speaking, everybody is right—except perhaps those who think they are the only ones who are right!

Allan Bloom in his perceptive book *The Closing of the American Mind* points out that with all of our so-called open-mindedness, the mind of the average American college student is closed. It is open only to one basic premise: that every view is as valid as any other. The student's mind is closed to the possibility of objective truth. Bloom writes, "There is no enemy other than the man who is not open to everything."[13]

What do the New Agers think of Jesus? He is a way to God. "He happens to be my point of access," said a woman advertising a seminar on miracles. "You may have a different point . . . you can keep your faith in Christ . . . we are just asking you to go beyond it."

As Norman Geisler says, the New Age Movement with its emphasis on the global unity of all beliefs and cultures "is like a cosmic sponge that absorbs all religions, cultures, and governments."[14] Pretending to accept anything, it becomes attractive to those who cling to their pride and choose whatever they want to believe.

However irrational this may be, it is in keeping with the present pride Americans have—pride in their pluralism. Anyone can believe whatever he wants to regardless of how absurd or contradictory. You take a belief from Christianity, a technique from Hinduism, and a dose of Tibetan magic, and you come up with your own private brand of religion.

Many who have borrowed helter-skelter from contradictory religions and worldviews may not even be aware of it. And, even more frightening, if it were pointed out to them, they may not even be bothered by it!

The steep price of such irrationality, however, is always deception. For if every worldview is equally right, it is also true that every worldview is equally wrong. Without a theological yardstick, absurdity, brutality, and despair are free to reign.

7. Counter setbacks with the reminder that we are all in a state of evolutionary transformation.

Sometimes the techniques do not work. Sometimes men so abuse one another that they act more like humans than gods. There are times when we cannot seem to get in touch with ourselves, even with the most expensive crystals and with the most diligent meditation. The love and harmony that seems to work so well along a seashore sometimes is difficult to detect back at the office. There are times when even New Agers get discouraged and forget that they are totally in charge of their own lives. When that happens, they need to fall back on the basics.

That's the time to remember that we are in a state of spiritual transformation. And such changes are painful. Multitudes of people are still unenlightened so we should not blame them for thinking in terms of absolutes and narrow-minded interests. They are neither right nor wrong, just unawakened to their true identity.

And sometimes even the enlightened have difficulty. These men and women have lived so long with negative thinking and religious prejudice that it is difficult to transcend the old ways of perceiving reality. The setbacks must be taken in stride with the fond hope that progress, though imperceptible, is being made nonetheless.

Running throughout these seven principles is the basic lie: you are God, and therefore you deserve the best. Look out for Number One. As Terry Cole-Whittaker put it, "Worship yourself. You are the light."[15] That line will sell in any country where people have broken the first commandment. When we turn from the true God, we eventually turn to ourselves.

A God we must have. The question is: which one?

Chapter Three

Meet the
"Evangelists"

*C*hristianity has its George Whitefield, D.L. Moody, and Billy Graham. These men and hundreds of evangelists like them through the centuries have derived their authority from a call from the living God.

Not to be outdone, Satan has his "evangelists" too. They hold high-priced seminars (learning the techniques of this "gospel" is not cheap), are courted for television talk shows, and write interesting books. They combine the new message with words of personal testimony. They say: "Look at what the New Age has done for me." The most powerful witness, we are told, is that of a changed life. Nothing like being able to say, "I once was a failure, struggling with bitterness and hurt, but now I am free. I can create my own reality; I can do whatever I want; I have found the resources within to climb the mountain. No longer do I fear death, for I have discovered that it does not exist."

There is power in the New Age Movement. Jeff is a

sandy-haired high school student who was heavily into drugs, alcohol, and punk rock. But he found no satisfaction until he found someone who exhibited a form of spirituality that was sufficient to change his life. The man was loving, kind, and filled with truth. With some instruction, Jeff had a profound spiritual experience. He "cleaned up his act," had a change of direction, and found new moral strength and peace. Jeff's experience sounded like that of a new convert to Jesus Christ.

The *Chicago Tribune* carried an article about Judith Kendall, a 43-year-old real estate developer who dropped out of Roman Catholicism to pursue the insights of the New Age Movement. She and a dozen others sit in a circle and read from a book that begins, "The world I see holds nothing that I want."[1] The book, *A Course in Miracles*, is a message supposedly delivered by Jesus to a scribe called Helen Schucman, a Jew-turned-atheist. It teaches that there are no sins; we must react to all the circumstances of life with love, not retaliation. Those who participate in groups that study these writings claim that they have, at last, found happiness. The *Tribune* reports, "There are no rules prohibiting smoking, drinking, dancing, swearing, drugs, or sex." The course deals with the realm of the ego, where judgments reign supreme and human bodies are temporal. The true world is spiritual.

Schucman, who died in 1981, began hearing an inner voice in 1965. She started recording what the voice said and thus the book was written. The voice said that this was "a required course in miracles."

And miracles do happen. Ask Judith Kendall, who says, "I was having trouble with my son. . . . He wanted to leave college. I was upset. . . . After reading the book and praying hard, I decided it best that he leave the house. So out he went. It wasn't done in anger. It was done in love and it wasn't easy for me."[2] Two weeks later he had a job and a place to live, returned to school, and is getting A's. She does not believe that this was an accident.

Miracles do occur, the head teacher says, when there is a "change in perception . . . in truth we are all spirit and the body is just an expression." A leaflet advertising a course in miracles says in bold print, I AM . . . YOU ARE . . . THE MIRACLES STAR!

A young Baptist woman, Cindy Williams, went through a difficult experience after a divorce and came to a New Age seminar for help. Though "leery" when she first entered, she now says it has changed her life. The problems of the world no longer bother her, and she strives to get in touch with her real self—the spiritual self. She keeps looking for those everyday miracles and says, "I've got my feet firmly planted on this illusion."[3]

Who are these recruiters, these "evangelists" who encourage others to plant their feet firmly on an illusion? It is difficult to compile such a list because their name is legion. Some defend the faith; others try to explain the phenomenon; still others simply share a word of testimony: "Once I was blind, but now I see."

Paul talks about those who claim to see the light, but walk in darkness: "Professing to be wise, they became fools. . . . For they exchanged the truth of God for a lie, and worshipped and served the creature rather than the Creator, who is blessed forever. Amen" (Romans 1:22, 25).

We've decided to limit our list to American New Age "evangelists" who have changed the truth of God into a lie. Gurus from India or other countries of the East have pockets of followers in the United States. But we are interested in those who have taken Eastern thought and translated it for Americans. This nation is attracted to those whose names are easy to pronounce, those who have made pantheism palatable to the Western mind. We're interested in what plays in Peoria.

Promoters of the Lie

These names are listed neither alphabetically nor in order of importance. Many others could be added, but here is a sample of some of the more influential spokespersons, most of whom are still living.

1. Marilyn Ferguson

Her book *The Aquarian Conspiracy*, published in 1980, gives us the rationale and agenda for the New Age Movement. She says, "A leaderless but powerful network is working to bring about radical change in the United States. Its members have broken with certain key elements of Western thought, and they may even have broken continuity with history."[4]

How powerful is the network? She says that there are legions of conspirators—in universities, hospitals, and schools. They are in the United States government, even at cabinet levels. "They have coalesced into small groups in every town and institution. . . . Some conspirators are keenly aware of the national, even international, scope of the movement and are active in linking others."[5]

In her chapter "Spiritual Adventure" she speaks about the "God of Force" and says that we are able to enter fully into the spirit of this impersonal god by returning to the ancient wisdom of the East. There we find a basis for optimism and spiritual adventure.

Ferguson's book has had a great impact because it systematically maps out the direction and basic beliefs of New Age thought. It details how the shift is taking place from West to East.

2. Shirley MacLaine

As an actress and author, Shirley MacLaine is presently one of the most influential "evangelists" for the New Age Movement. Several books command our attention. *Out on a Limb*[6] was published in 1983 and relates the beginning of her transformation into the spiritual realm. She began searching for knowledge about herself and the unseen world. Soon she had a guided tour of what she describes as "dimensions of time and space that heretofore, for me, belonged in science fiction or what I would describe as the occult."

In her search she received help from two spirits by way of a trance or medium. They taught God is a force or divine energy, and Jesus is a highly evolved human being.

Her second book *Dancing in the Light*[7] continues the saga. She exercises with yoga, uses crystals for spiritual power, and chants Hindu mantras. Now she has progressed to the point of believing that each individual is God. Her spirit guides inform her, "If everyone was taught one basic spiritual law, your world would be a happier, healthier place. And that law is this: everyone is God. Everyone." Other books have followed, giving a further description of her absorption with the occult.

Perhaps MacLaine had the greatest impact on Americans when her best-selling books were dramatized on television in a popular miniseries in November 1986. Millions followed the story that was, in effect, a sales pitch for basic Hindu philosophy. She also holds high-priced seminars, which have caused one writer to observe that she may be out on a limb, but the tree she is shaking is full of money.[8]

The readability of these books and the lure of personal testimony via television have created a maximum "evangelistic" impact. MacLaine unashamedly says she is out to save souls. She asks questions that most of us have wondered about and then gives the New Age answers. The impression is that those who are truly thoughtful could appreciate the insight from the spiritual, metaphysical reality. After all, since most of us have a lot of problems in life and we all crave a spiritual solution, why not give this new approach a decent try? Thus Americans are "softened" toward a destructive religion based on Eastern thought.

3. Napoleon Hill

His book *Think and Grow Rich*[9] has sold millions of copies. It is the basis for many of the motivational seminars that are held for the business community in the United States. And just what does Hill teach that gives him the distinction of being a powerful advocate of the New Age philosophy?

The secret lies in the power of the mind, the ability anyone has to develop his or her raw potential. But, as in all mind-expanding techniques, there is also the power of the occult. In the last chapter we pointed out that Hill identifies the source of his ideas as "unseen friends," apparently unaware that he is in contact with evil spirits.

What is his great secret? *Anything the human mind can believe, the human mind can achieve.* This is the destructive lie that undergirds the Human Potential Movement. These ideas have also been taken by Christians who have tried to integrate New Age thought with the Bible. The implications of this will be seen more fully in a later chapter.

4. Jose Silva

This man has become popular because of his firm conviction that anyone who will take his 48-hour course in mind control will be able to develop psychic powers. You will be taught how to enter a higher state of consciousness and in that way tap into the higher intelligence of the universe. You will be taught how to invite psychic guides into your life to help you solve your problems. Clients can have out-of-body experiences and receive communication from the minds of other men, whether they are dead or alive. And what is more, Silva believes that God sent Jesus to this world to teach us all this. After all, did He not alter physical reality by changing water into wine, and one loaf of bread into many?

To keep us from thinking that this is nothing but ancient witchcraft in modern American dress, the explanation for the power of mind over matter is couched in *scientific* terms. The mind radiates "spiritual energy" that has the ability to alter reality. Also, information from other people's minds has been programmed on inanimate matter and animate matter. Thus the spiritual energy of the mind is able to decode this programmed material. So strictly speaking, the person who takes the Silva Mind Control Course is not contacting dead people, but rather decoding messages that were programmed when they were still alive.

Silva believes that all the school children of America should be taught these basic mind-control techniques. A grade school teacher in Buffalo claims that these teachings are having a profound and beneficial effect on her students.

Interestingly, Silva admits that we might not always get the spirit guides we invite into our minds. But he claims to be able to detect a false medium from a true one by the information that is received from the entity. A reliable guide is one that will help solve people's problems; a false one gives information that is not helpful. To quote him: "But if you get information to solve problems, where people are suffering, and you do alleviate that suffering and you correct the problem, who cares where the information comes from? The idea is to get it any way you can to stop a problem and forget everything else."[10]

Apparently Jose Silva has forgotten that demons often give helpful information for purposes of deception and can at times parrot excellent theology—as when they confessed to Christ that He was the Son of God.

5. Terry Cole-Whittaker

This woman had a great religious following in California, teaching the gospel of prosperity. Her message was simple: go after wealth, power, and success. Stop feeling guilty for having more in a have-not world.

But on March 17, 1985 she announced to her congregation and television audience that she was leaving the ministry. In her final message she told how she had surrendered to Jesus and received peace and love. But she went on to clarify, "This doesn't mean that you have to surrender to Jesus. Not at all. It wasn't Jesus that made the difference, it was my willingness to trust in a higher power. . . . "[11]

A series of experiences led her into Hinduism and other New Age beliefs. She has spoken to a 35,000-year-old entity named Ramtha and believes we can take away our guilt feelings by reprogramming the way we think. She is optimistic about the coming new world where there will be such peace and love that money will not even be necessary. Her most popular book is entitled *The Inner Path from Where You Are to Where You Want to Be.*

6. Werner Erhard

One of the most important mind-control movements is called *Forum*, formerly *est* (Erhard Seminar Training). This is an intensive 60-hour seminar of psychological indoctrination designed to change the way we perceive reality. In 1982 there were 300,000 *est* graduates and their numbers have been rapidly expanding. Erhard's goal is to put *est* into education. Indeed, the schools, the prisons, and businesses provide many opportunities to prove the benefits of his program.

Erhard had a conversion experience of enlightenment while driving his car in California. After that, his interest in Eastern occultism intensified; he has made trips to the East to study with Zen masters.

Erhard states, "We want nothing short of total transformation—an alteration of substance, not a change of form."[12] All this is accomplished by wearing people down, by group dynamics, and by breaking down all defenses.

The training is unashamedly religious: you are God and live in a perfect universe. You no longer have to be concerned about the suffering and needs of those about you, for they too are God and responsible for their own destiny. As for rules about life, Erhard has but one: life has no rules.

7. Edgar Cayce

An encyclopedia on occult phenomena calls Cayce "possibly the greatest occult diagnostician of modern times."[13] Though he died in his hometown of Hopkinsville, Kentucky in 1945, his legacy as a miracle-worker lives on.

As a child, Cayce is said to have spoken with an angel and had a series of visions of his dead grandfather. To diagnose sicknesses, he would go into a trance state and receive information that was valuable to patients. Predictably, people came from all over the world to receive his help. According to his own records, he helped treat 30,000 people over a span of 43 years. He also claimed clairvoyance and is said to have discovered the identity of a murderer while in a trance.

Cayce believed in reincarnation and that he himself once had been reincarnated as the Egyptian high priest Ra Ta. During that life he helped build the Great Pyramid. In another life he was a soldier of Troy and helped defend the besieged citadel. When the city fell, he committed suicide.

But there is more: Cayce taught that Jesus was incarnated as the biblical Adam around 12,000 B.C. Naturally this leads to the assumption that Jesus committed the first sin. So when Cayce was asked, "When did the knowledge come to Jesus that He was to be the Saviour of the world?" he answered, "When He fell in Eden."

Cayce appealed to millions because he skillfully combined theosophy, pyramidology, Hinduism, and Christianity. He published a journal called *The New Tomorrow*. The Cayce Foundation of America continues to honor him, and thousands of followers attempt to carry out what he has begun.

Understandably, Shirley MacLaine quotes Cayce as an authority on channeling, reincarnation, and the like.

New Age Movements

In addition to this selected list of individuals, most of whom are present-day "evangelists" for the New Age Movement, there are a number of philosophical and religious movements (past or present) that basically teach the four spiritual flaws detailed in the first chapter of this book.[14]

Here is a partial list:

1. *Transcendentalism* introduced Eastern thought into America as far back as the 1800s. Two of its early adherents, Henry David Thoreau and Ralph Waldo Emerson,

were basically pantheists influenced by the mysticism of the East. Like the New Agers of today, they were eclectic, accepting or discarding whatever they wished from Eastern thought.

2. *New Thought*, often associated with the writings of the Swedish philosopher Emanuel Swedenborg (1688-1772), also became popular in America in the 19th century, brought to this continent by the Austrian physician Franz Mesmer (1734-1815). Mesmer, from whom we get the word *mesmerize*, was the father of modern hypnosis.

Christian Science, based upon the writings of Mary Baker Eddy, grew out of the spiritism of the New Thought Movement. The basic premise is that all that exists is mind; matter is basically illusionary. Since thought is the final reality, the mind can create whatever reality it wishes— hence the famous expression, "Mind over matter."

3. *Theosophy*, a name popularized by the Theosophical Society founded in 1875, stands in the Eastern tradition of Hinduism and spiritual thought. Robert Burrows, a researcher for the Spiritual Counterfeits Project, characterizes it as a "dizzy blend of Western occultism and Eastern mysticism."[15]

4. *Psychoanalysis*, which arrived in America at the end of the 19th century, was heavily influenced by occult theorists. Carl Jung (1875-1961) believed in the deity of man and accepted the mind-expanding insights gleaned from psychics and occult teachers. He had many paranormal experiences and attributed his book *Seven Sermons to the Dead* to automatic writing, a phenomena often found in occult circles.

The fact that these "evangelists" and movements are receiving such popular support in America is an indication of how far this nation has drifted back to paganism. The allegiance of millions is being openly courted by the media and respected leaders in this nation. Multitudes are stepping into Satan's kingdom by accepting the basic lies.

Given the widespread acclaim enjoyed by Satan's "evangelists," every true believer should be challenged by the opportunity of witnessing to the transforming power of Christ. The true church has often been paralyzed in its witness because of the notion that the job rests only with certain "called" evangelists. But the New Testament teaches that *every believer is to be a witness* (Acts 1:8); we have the responsibility of sharing the good news of the Gospel and seeing it work.

Christ is stronger than the satanic mind-control techniques promoted by these pseudo-evangelists. If we think that those who are involved in Eastern religions cannot be converted to Christ, we insult God. Is the devil's gospel stronger than that of the ascended Christ? God has given us an opportunity to compare the benefits of the two gospels—the false and the true.

Now we turn to a more detailed analysis of the Four Spiritual Flaws and see how they are packaged for American audiences.

Chapter Four

Pantheism:
The First Spiritual Flaw

*I*f it is true, as A.W. Tozer has said, that no religion can rise higher than its conception of God, we must be as clear as possible about what kind of God is accepted by the New Age Movement. We've already learned that the New Age is built on a spiritual perception of reality. Terms such as *psychic, metaphysical, mental,* and *spiritual* continually reoccur. Whereas secular humanism teaches that there is no spiritual dimension to the universe, the New Age Movement believes that reality is primarily, if not exclusively, spiritual. Indeed, the universe is populated with spirits (entities) and the human mind can be put in touch with the mystical oneness of all things. This is a world of miracles and out-of-body experiences. And it is a world where you can encounter God in everyone and everything.

The Three Views of God
Since the beginning of time, three primary conceptions of God have vied for the allegiance of men.

Theism is the belief that God is the creator and sustainer of the universe. The Judeo-Christian tradition best exemplifies this understanding of who God is; He is personal, powerful, and independent of the universe. He can, to some degree, be known to mankind in this life and will be forever worshipped and served by those in heaven. Because He is both personal and just, He will eventually bring every individual into personal judgment so that righteousness will eventually prevail.

Atheism is the view that there is no God. The final reality is believed to be matter, not spirit. In fact, there is no spiritual aspect to the world. There are no souls, no angels, demons, or mystical realities. Atheism denies the possibility of life after death and insists that miracles cannot occur. Perhaps atheism is best expressed in the now famous line of Carl Sagan in his book *Cosmos*: "The cosmos is all there ever was and is, all there will ever be."

Understandably, atheists are opposed to the New Age Movement. They see it as another futile attempt by man to formulate answers to ultimate questions, answers that are simply not available. Atheist Paul Kurtz debunks all paranormal claims and "occult superstitions."[1] His targets, he says, are psychic phenomena, UFO abductions, and various New Age practices and practitioners. Kurtz believes the movement accepts uncorroborated claims made by gurus, seers, and prophets who promise people anything. So he campaigns against astrology and other occult practices. Atheists believe that the New Age Movement may have some value in helping superstitious people, but its concept of a spiritual dimension to the universe must be rejected.

Pantheism is a conception of God that pervades the New Age Movement. It is most easily defined as the belief that "God is all and all is God." The word *pan* means "all" and as such refers to the idea that all that exists is God; there are merely different levels of existence that correspond to different levels of divinity. The lowest level is matter, then comes the vegetable kingdom, followed by the animal kingdom, and finally, mankind. But everything is God. Nature is God; you are God; I am God. God is all there is.

For the pantheist, the final reality in the universe is spiritual. In fact, matter is really an illusion. Borrowing from the Eastern religion of Hinduism, the New Agers believe that we must deny the existence of the material universe to escape into the world of mind, which is in touch with the spiritual universe that is truly real.

God is an impersonal force; God is energy, and energy is God. This redefinition of God, we are told, is supported by the scientific studies in quantum mechanics. Fritjof Capra wrote *The Tao of Physics* to demonstrate how the two foundations of 20th-century physics (quantum theory and relativity theory) both force us to see the world very much like a Hindu or Buddhist or Taoist sees it. There is no such thing as solid matter, just energy. It follows that what we call solid matter is really an illusion. So—the argument goes—science, Hinduism, and the New Age Movement ultimately agree that there is only substance in the universe, namely a force or energy that comprises all there is. Interestingly, Capra says his studies came about as a result of a mystical experience in which he felt cosmic energy and knew this was the "Dance of Shiva," the Lord of Dancers worshipped by the Hindus.[2]

We should note in passing that even if science concludes that what we call matter is in fact energy, this would not prove that this energy is God. Nor would it erase our normal experiences of "material objects." Science, if anything, has shown that nature acts rationally; that is, purposefully. The most rational explanation for this is the doctrine of Creation, not the belief in an impersonal force that acts randomly and without intelligence.

God, then, is the great IT. To quote the words of New Ager Dick Sutphen, "In the beginning there existed the great energy, the gestalt. We call it God, but any other name would serve just as well."

In India the impersonalization of God is cleverly promoted. Biblical statements such as "God is love" or "God is wisdom" are reversed to read "love is God" and "wisdom is God." By changing the word order, there is a profound change in meaning. God is depersonalized; He is reduced to the collective wisdom and love found in mankind. God is not thought of as having an existence independent of the universe.

Closer to home, the Eastern idea of God as an impersonal force was introduced to millions of Americans in the *Star Wars* trilogy. George Lucas, who produced these movies, admits that they convey a religious message. "There is a God and there is both a good side and a bad side. You have a choice between them, but the world works better if you're on the good side."[3] By falling in love with the characters in these movies many Americans were being introduced to a concept of God that will eventually ruin our society. If you think that statement is too strong, just consider some of the implications of this worldview.

The Implications of Pantheism
1. Man is his own savior.
Christianity and the New Age Movement clash at every point. But nowhere is this seen more clearly than in the doctrine of salvation. Christianity teaches that man fell into sin and needs to be rescued by the death, resurrection, and ascension of Christ. He paid a penalty for sinners so that through faith they can be restored to God. Man is the sinner; God is the Saviour.

Pantheism teaches that there never was a fall. What happened was this: at one time matter and mind were united as one; they were one continuous, unified force called God. But then a separation occurred. Matter and mind still are God, but they parted one from the other. *Salvation means that these two aspects of God become united once more.* This happens through meditation and the mystical experience that causes us to lose our personal identity.

Think through the words of Nikos Kazantzakis, who incidentally is also the author of *The Last Temptation of Christ*: "It is not God who will save us—it is we who will save God, by battling, by creating and transmuting matter into spirit."[4]

Shirley MacLaine would agree. She says that the word *atonement* means "At-one-ment with the original creator or with the original creation."[5] We are both creator and creation, and we can bring the two closer together. The possibility of atonement rests with us.

Man saves God!

Christianity says that man fell and God redeems him; pantheism says that *God* fell and *man* redeems Him! Man redeems God by bringing the material aspect of deity back into harmony with the spiritual.

Here is a challenge. Read all the New Age literature you can and see if you can find a single instance where it tells you that you need help from God to experience the transformation of consciousness we are told is so necessary for a satisfactory life. In every case, you will find that we have the potential within ourselves to experience the perfection we need. The message is: *you are God, so save yourself!*

Clearly the New Testament Gospel stands in strong opposition to the new "gospel" of pantheism. I'm reminded of the words of G.K. Chesterton: "When a man ceases to believe in God, he does not believe in nothing. He believes in anything!"

He will even believe in his own divinity!

2. Pantheism destroys morality.

If it is true that God is everything, it follows that God is also evil. That's why Hinduism teaches that good and evil are only illusions; they only *appear* to differ from one another. Allan Watts, who is credited with making Zen Buddhism palatable to Americans, explains it this way: life is like a play where you see good and bad men in conflict on the stage, but behind the curtain, they are the best of friends. Backstage, God and Satan go hand in hand. Only the uninformed differentiate between good and evil. To quote Yen-Men, one of the great Eastern teachers, "If you wish the plain truth, be not concerned about right and wrong. The conflict between right and wrong is the sickness of the mind."[6]

Charles Manson will not go down in history as a great theologian but, because he had adopted the pantheism of the East, the mass murderer asked, "If God is all, what is evil?" At the heart of pantheism is a denial of evil, since both good and evil can be ascribed to God. In fact, since God is all and all is God, it follows that the Easterners teach that God is male and female; plus and minus; darkness and light; he is perfection and what is sometimes wrongly called sin. In this universe, everything is moral, for everything is God.

Since evil does not exist, it follows that man's problem is not sin but ignorance. All that we need is enlightenment. The goal of transcendental meditation, so popular among the educated in America, leads inevitably to the denial of the distinction between good and evil. TM teaches that we should come to the point where we no longer think of anything in particular. When the mind is blank, free from the illusions of right and wrong, and accepts the illusionary character of the material world, then one has achieved a high degree of spiritual reality. The Buddha who sits under the tree, uncaring, unfeeling, and unthinking, has finally reached the perfect spiritual state.

Pantheism with its denial of morality is actually more dangerous than the secular humanism we have all heard so much about. Inconsistent as the humanists are, they still wish to cling to some of the standards of the Judeo-Christian tradition. Atheism still teaches the need for morality of some sort. But Eastern thought logically abolishes morality altogether.

Since morality plays such an important role in every religion, a separate chapter will be devoted to it later in this book.

3. Pantheism devalues human life.

Obviously, if everything is God, it follows that man is God too. In fact, this is the most basic doctrine of the New Age Movement. On the surface it would seem that pantheism exalts mankind to a high position in the universe, but as we shall see in a moment quite the opposite is true. Maharishi, often known as the father of transcendental meditation, said, "Be still and know that you are God."

Terry Cole-Whittaker, who at one time professed to be a Christian evangelist, said, "You are God, I am God. Together we are God. And together with our own consciousness, awakening, and choice we create the kingdom of God. Worship yourself, you are the light."[7]

That is high praise. Now that man has proclaimed himself as God we would think that he would be in a position to live up to his exalted responsibility. But let's take a closer look at what happens when pantheism is consistently applied.

Yes, man is God, but so are the animals such as the cows and the ants; so are the trees and the weeds and the stones and the ground. Everything is God. *To say that man is God is hardly a compliment if the same can be said for worms and thistles!*

India is a country where these ideas have been rather consistently applied. Has pantheism resulted in human dignity and a high concept of man? No, it has not, and for some obvious reasons. In saying that everything is God, man has lost his uniqueness; he has been reduced to the same level as the plants and animals around him.

Shirley MacLaine got into Eastern religions because she found conditions in India so depressing. Starvation, poverty, and death are difficult for us to accept, so one is tempted to construct an independent reality in the mind. Though the outward circumstances are painful and hopeless, the mind can be free. If I am just a mind and not a body, why should I care whether I starve or freeze to death?

But what has caused the food shortages in India? It is

not because the country is poor in natural resources; indeed, it is one of the richest countries in the world. The greatest source of the problem is the pantheism of Hinduism, the conception of God now promoted in the United States by the New Age Movement.

In India you are not to kill rats because these rodents are, of course, God. The July 1977 issue of *National Geographic* magazine estimated that 20 percent of India's food supply is being consumed by rats. This was enough grain, the article went on to say, to fill a freight train that would extend from Los Angeles to New York City. Monkeys destroy an estimated 15 percent of India's food, and another 15 percent is fed to nonproductive cows. These animals are more important than starving infants.[8]

And why not? Remember if everything is God, then everything should get equal treatment. Rats cannot be exterminated; cattle cannot be killed for food; trees cannot be cut down to serve the needs of man. So pathetic is the degeneration of the people there that a recent Indian prime minister recommended regularly drinking a cup of cow urine to cleanse the body. Thus, *in pantheism animals are not elevated to the status of man; man must of necessity be reduced to the status of animals.*

Advocates of the animal rights movement often teach that animals should be given the same rights as humans. On a Christmas morning, members of the Animal Liberation Front stole 11 German shepherds and a collie being used in heart research at Harbor-UCLA Medical Center near Los Angeles. After the break-in a phone call was received asking, "Why don't you save the dogs and do research on yourselves or welfare recipients?"

Whenever we give the same rights to animals as we do to humans, man is brought down to the level of the animal kingdom. Whenever there is a conflict of rights, as there must be, man must be willing to defer to the animals. What right does one god have to trample on the rights of another god? Thus cows can be fed while babies starve.

If you think that such pantheistic ideas have little respect in the United States, consider this article from the March 1986 *Farm Journal* entitled, "Where Dairy Cows Find Nirvana." A cow named Dwarka and several of her kind in Juniata County, Pennsylvania are pampered and talked to just like members of the family. These cows need not fear that they will be led to the slaughterhouse. When their milking days are over they are free to retire, lounge around the barn, and "swap bull stories." The article humorously describes how Americans can, for a donation of $3,000, adopt a cow for life. "As a reward the commune will send the donor an 8 x 10 color photograph of the cow, a gold certificate, and sweets made from the cow's milk. Of course there will be periodic reports of the cow's progress, and a get-acquainted vacation weekend at the farm comes with the price of the ticket!"[9]

We smile at the story, and fortunately such investments are not yet common among the American public. Probably such Hindu beliefs will never gain popularity in the West. But in a pantheistic world the idea of giving cows equal status with humans is not foolish—it is just the logical consequence of a wrong view of God. *Whenever man worships nature, he ends up being in subjection to it.*

Not only does pantheism make man suffer because it brings him down to the level of animals, but the animals suffer too. For example, the cows of India are not as well fed as those in the Netherlands. Since the latter nation does not believe that cows are gods, it has developed a method of breeding and care that has resulted in some of the most productive cattle in the world. When man takes responsibility as the custodian of nature, he has the ability to help himself as well as animals, plants, and the general environment.

Here in the United States, the environmental movement often is used to promote a pantheistic worldview. That we should do all we can to protect the environment goes without saying, but when we hear expressions such as "Mother

Earth" we must look for clues to see whether this is just an affectionate reference to the earth that all of us depend on, or if, in fact, it promotes the belief that the earth is God.

The Sierra Club's Environmental Health Sourcebook called *Well Body, Well Earth* leaves us in no doubt about the answer. In this book we are taught how to contact the spirit of Mother Earth. After learning how to relax and make contact, the writers advise us:

> You are now in a deeply relaxed state, a level of consciousness at which your mind feels peaceful and open. At this level you can be in touch with those forces in the universe that stabilize systems and encourage health and well-being. You can now experience the visualizations vividly and pleasantly. . . . When you are done with your conversation with the spirit of the living Earth, say goodbye to it, just as you would say goodbye upon parting from a friend. . . . The more you contact the voice of the living Earth, and evaluate what it says, the easier it will become for you to contact it and trust what it provides.[10]

So Mother Earth is really a part of the divine, the force or energy which we can tap for information and our own well-being. Here we have basic occultism wearing the mask of environmentalism. Pantheism, a destructive religious worldview, is being sold to those who care about the proper use of our natural resources. The concern is of course legitimate; the solution is not.

4. Pantheism hinders science.

Pantheism and the scientific method are fundamentally incompatible. Pantheism calls on us to *worship* nature, for it is in fact God; science calls us to *work with* nature and to use it, since it was created for man's benefit. When God put man in the Garden, he was to keep it and till it—nature was under man's control. This does not mean that man is to squander these resources; indeed he is accountable to

God for how he exercises his stewardship of the earth.

Pantheism denies the reality of nature, claiming that nature is ultimately illusionary. Everything can be reduced to the force, the impersonal energy called God. Science, on the other hand, believes in the reality of the natural world. What is more, this world behaves according to some very regular patterns (laws) that can be used for man's good.

The question of whether nature should be feared and worshipped or whether it is to be used and harnessed is fundamental for Western society. Our standard of living is based on the Judeo-Christian belief that nature is not God; it was created by God for the careful use and benefit of man. The West has achieved a higher standard of living, not because of intellectual brilliance but because of a worldview that has set man free from nature worship; he is free to work with nature rather than yoke himself to nature by claiming the deity of all things.

Perhaps the contrast between the two worldviews can be best illustrated by observing some scenery just outside Madras, India. If we as Westerners woke up some morning and discovered a five-foot anthill in our backyard, we would soon take some measures to control the ants. Soon that anthill would be leveled and the remaining ants would have to go elsewhere to build their home and multiply their species. But outside Madras the anthill is not destroyed. To the contrary, a shrine is built around it and worshippers come to bow down before it. After all, that is what we would expect from a pantheist—to worship ants, rats, or trees. That, after all, is to worship God.

We must ask: what should our attitude toward nature be? Is it to be revered as God, or is it to be carefully used for man's benefit? The continuation of modern science hinges on the answer.

Pantheism's Grand Lie

As we wrote in chapter 1, the seeds of pantheism were sown in the Garden of Eden when the serpent convinced

Adam and Eve that disobedience against God would really result in their being like God. Down through the ages, men and women have echoed that lie. Indeed, in Shirley MacLaine's TV miniseries there is one particularly dramatic scene when she is initiated into the understanding that the human soul is one with the divine being. As she and her spiritual adviser stand on Malibu Beach with their arms flung open to the cosmos, they joyously shout, "I AM GOD! I AM GOD!" A channeler through whom the ancient entity Ramtha speaks said on the Merv Griffin show in October 1985 that the most important message she had for people was, "What is termed God is within your being . . . and that which is called Christ is within your being . . . and when you know you are God, you will find joy."

The belief "There is no God" has now been transformed into "I am God." At the end of the age the lie of man's deity will be widely believed. Paul says that when Antichrist comes, he will work in accord with Satan. He will claim to be God, and the world will believe him because "God will send upon them a deluding influence so that they might believe what is false" (2 Thessalonians 2:11). What is the lie that the world will be prepared to believe? It is that this man is God. If I am God and you are God, accepting Antichrist who makes this claim with an air of finality will not be difficult.

Pantheism denies morality, degrades man, and inhibits science. But, most of all, it is the scheme of Satan to get man to believe the Grand Lie. Sinful man, already filled with selfishness, has infatuated himself. He seeks enlightenment, but not forgiveness. He now has a rationale for self-absorption and unconditional self-acceptance.

But a lie it is. Man is not God; God is God. He is not an impersonal force; He is not indifferent to good and evil. He sees the sparrow fall to the ground and knows the number of hairs on our heads. Though we are born under the condemnation of sin, there is a way out of our predicament. For God is "gracious and compassionate, slow to anger, and abounding in lovingkindness" (Nehemiah 9:17). This God can be contacted through the historical Christ who said, "I am the way, and the truth, and the life; no one comes to the Father but through Me" (John 14:6).

Pantheism, far from exalting man, degrades him; theism exalts him to his rightful place in the world. He is not God, but a steward of God's world.

The Final Conflict

Satan is preparing for his final assault on God. The Antichrist will proclaim his own deity and invite the world to worship him. *And worship him they will.* He will give to those who follow him a mark, a sign of initiation, proving that they have passed the test of allegiance.

What about those who do not accept the grand lie of man's divinity, those who still maintain faith in the living and true God? They will be persecuted and put to death. "And it was given to him to make war with the saints and to overcome them; and authority over every tribe and people and tongue and nation was given to him" (Revelation 13:7).

Antichrist will hold all the economic cards in his hands. Those who do not do business with him will be systematically eliminated.

The final conflict will come down to this question: who is God?

There will be moments when it will appear as if Satan will win over the Almighty. Multitudes will do his bidding. The recruits he has carefully deceived throughout the years will stand by his side, believing with all their hearts that their optimistic dreams are being fulfilled.

But Satan's successes will be short-lived. The deity of man will once and for all be proven as the Grand Lie. God, His truth, and His people will prevail.

Chapter Five

Reincarnation:
The Second Spiritual Flaw

*S*hirley MacLaine confidently teaches that we can now eliminate the fear of death from the minds of all Americans and indeed from the consciousness of the whole world. Death, says the influential actress, simply does not exist.

This is welcome news. Hamlet, you will recall, had no such assurance, but wondered aloud about the possible terrors that awaited him if he committed suicide:

> For in that sleep of death what dreams may come
> When we have shuffled off this mortal coil . . .

What evidence is there that Hamlet's fears were unfounded? And, if death does in fact not exist, how then should we understand the transition from this life to the next?

Shirley MacLaine finds that both questions are answered in the ancient religion of Hinduism. Through contact with entities in the spirit world, she has discovered that she was a princess in Atlantis, an Inca in Peru, and even once a child raised by elephants. In some previous existences she was male; in others she was female. She believes that we go around perhaps 50 or 100 times in a cycle of spiritual evolution.

Reincarnation, according to the New Agers, has several advantages over Christianity. For one thing, it eliminates the fear of death; what we call death is nothing more than a transition to a new existence where nothing fundamental has changed. Second, it gives a rationale for the problem of evil. At last we find out why tragedy happens to some and not to others. While Christianity teaches that this world is filled with injustice, reincarnation teaches that all things operate according to the law of karma. There is an identifiable reason for evil in the world. Amid all the pain and trauma we endure, we can take heart.

There are three basic pieces to the puzzle of reincarnationism. Let's look at them one at a time.

Pantheism

In the last chapter we stressed that the New Age Movement grows out of the Eastern belief of pantheism—all is God and God is all. God is the force, the impersonal energy that pervades the universe, or rather, that *is* the universe. God is both good and evil, and because we are God, or at least part of God, we too have good and the illusion of evil.

For the pantheist, reality is spiritual, not material. In fact, matter, like evil, is an illusion that the faithful come to disregard as a distraction in the path to true oneness.

So much for the first piece of the puzzle.

Transmigration of Souls

Long before Charles Darwin, the Hindus had their own understanding of evolution, the notion of the gradual development of the soul to higher forms. This evolution can be illustrated by a series of continuous circles, gradually working up the scale. There is neither a beginning nor an end, but an endless process of refinement and perfection. The system slowly but surely purges out the weak, the unfit, the undesirable.

Darwin, who applied a similar theory to the natural world, gave his first edition of *The Origin of Species* the subtitle "The Preservation of the Favored Races in the Struggle for Life." He believed that the favored races would eventually eliminate the inferior races of the earth. This teaching agrees with the theory of spiritual evolution taught in Hinduism.

Reincarnationism holds that plants, animals, and human life are so interrelated that souls are capable of "transmigrating" from one form of life to another. One could have been a plant or an animal in a previous existence.

Even though New Agers believe nature is illusionary, they still generally accept Darwin's evolutionary hypothesis. But they also accept an even more important spiritual evolution through which souls are perfected. On the one hand, everyone is God, but yet we are all also in the "process of becoming." The evil is being replaced with good. Our problem is that we do not have enough time to achieve this higher goodness in one lifetime. Shirley MacLaine says it's like show business—you just keep doing it until "you get it right."

So souls play a kind of musical chairs with the various bodies in the world. In this life you may be one person, but another in the next. Ever onward and upward, the process moves relentlessly forward as we better ourselves with each cycle.

Reincarnationism also teaches a kind of *devolution* as well as *evolution*. This means that if you accumulate some bad karma you could regress in your journey toward the nothingness of nirvana. You could be a spider or a worm in the life to come. But this aspect of Hinduism is conveniently omitted when marketed for American audiences. The mood in the West is upbeat and optimistic. Everyone is making progress as they complete their cycles. With each round, a better form of life is reached.

Some Americans are not quite so optimistic. The popular talk-show host Morton Downey says, "I've got to recycle myself somehow . . . I am energy, I know that . . . I don't know if I will make it to heaven or whether I will become a battery in someone's flashlight, but I believe I'll go on."[1]

If the New Agers are to be believed, he need not worry about becoming a battery in someone's flashlight. The optimistic reincarnationists say that the cycle is ever upward and onward, ever wiser and more complete. No need to worry about devolution on this side of the ocean.

Now for the third piece of the puzzle.

Karma

The doctrine of karma refers to an irrevocable law that *everyone gets what he or she deserves*. There is an impersonal force in the world that causes us to build future debits and credits based on our behavior. The quality of life experienced in the next life depends on our present actions and behavior. Evil is always punished in the life to come; good is always rewarded. The more the soul renounces the material world by putting away its lust and pride, the more it loses itself in "the force" or "universal consciousness," the freer it will become from this horrible material world. The final outcome will be nirvana, the salvation of the soul by being absorbed into the one eternal reality.

This means that all people begin life at different levels. No one can claim equal rights. Some, because of sin, have forfeited all privileges, while others, because of good works, have been born into high positions and are well on their way to the escape of nirvana, the destination for the privileged few (though eventually all will probably make it).

The best application of this theory can be seen in the caste system in which the weak must serve the strong. The lower exists for the benefit of the higher.

India is rigidly divided into four major castes. Those who are on the lowest end of the scale are so polluted that they cannot even belong to one of these four groups. They are called "untouchables"—outcasts. Each of the four castes has its own function, which reflects a rigid division of labor. Keep in mind the basic principle: the poor exist to serve the rich. The polluted keep the streets clean for the holy; the untouchables collect the filth to serve those who are further along in their journey to perfection. *Although the lower always serve the higher; the higher are under no obligation to serve the lower.* Why should the rich help the poor if the poor are only receiving what they have coming to them? They are just reaping what they have sown.

The highest caste is the Brahmin. He is considered sacred; the worst imaginable crime is to murder him. If you assault him, you must be put to death; if you slander him, your tongue is cut off. His property is so sacred that the king cannot tax it. The Brahmin is served by those beneath him.

The Brahmin is free, however, to assault a man who is of a lower caste. If the Brahmin is upbraided for it, it is because he has polluted himself by touching someone who is defiled. This explains why wealthy men are able to leave an opulent hotel and walk out on the streets, stepping over beggars and starving children without so much as a twinge of conscience or a spark of compassion. In fact, if they were to alleviate the suffering of the poor, they just might be interfering with the delicate balance of justice administered by karma. Remember, everyone gets precisely what he or she deserves.

Ghandi, in his earlier days, steadfastly resisted any attempts to give the Untouchables recognition. In 1931, the British wanted to give the Untouchables representation in the Indian national legislature as a kind of affirmative action program. Ghandi was dead set against this move and almost starved himself to death to block such a humanitarian gesture. Needless to say, this scene was omitted from the motion picture *Ghandi*, a movie shrewdly designed to give him favorable publicity in the West.[2]

True, India is changing after centuries of such gross injustice. Pressure from Britain and other Western nations is causing the caste system to show some cracks. But changes can only come about as Hinduism begins to lose its grip on the lives of the people there.

Shirley MacLaine believes, however, that karma is a better explanation for the problem of evil than that offered by Christianity. It explains why some children are deformed or crippled in this life. It also explains why some are granted good health and are relatively free from trouble.

Let's think of the implications: here are several suffering children. One has leukemia, another is a cripple, and a third is dying of starvation. You want to help these children understand themselves better, so you say, "You are getting exactly what you deserve; you have these problems because you committed some great sins in a previous existence."

Here is another child, a four-year-old boy abused by an angry father with a lit cigarette. A six-year-old girl is beaten, her arms and legs broken by an angry and irrational mother. You say to them, "You were not the victims of injustice. You got exactly what you had coming to you because of sins you committed in a previous life—sins you cannot remember."

The bottom line is that karma teaches that *there is no injustice in the world.* Everything that happens is always because of some previous evil or good that was done. In fact, karma is meticulous in its distribution of justice. Whatever happens to you is determined *exclusively* by the deeds of your previous existence. The fact that you don't remember what you did is irrelevant. You are responsible anyway. Because karma doles out justice with such fine-tuned accuracy, *whatever is, should be.*

Reincarnationism has other implications. Shirley MacLaine found out that some women were males in previous existences. It dawned on her that she might have stumbled on an explanation that would help us understand our present society. After being told that she was a male at least twice in previous lives she asked her entity (an unseen spirit) whether this could be a metaphysical explanation for homosexuality. "I mean, maybe a soul makes a rocky transition from a female to a male body, for instance, and there is leftover emotional residue and attraction from the previous incarnation?"[3] John, the entity with whom she spoke, agreed; all souls are basically the same because elements of both sexes are present.

MacLaine also surmises that reincarnationism may explain why we are attracted to certain people. For example, she had an affair with a Russian lover and concluded that one reason why she may have had an immediate attraction to him is because he may have been her son in a previous existence. This might also be used to explain why a man suddenly finds himself attracted to another man's wife—he may have been married to the woman in a previous existence.

Yes, behavior such as adultery can be interpreted according to the laws of karmic necessity. Gina Cerminara gives some examples and explains:

> In short, such cases would indicate that the infidelity of the mate sometimes occurs through karmic necessity. . . . John's unfaithfulness to Mary may be due to the fact that Mary deserves this treament because of her unfaithfulness to Claudius in ancient Rome, but on the other hand his philandering may stem from Mary's failing in the present; the infidelity may be no more than a contemporary reaction to a contemporary instigation—a case of quick karma.[4]

And if karma can be used to justify adultery, why cannot it be pressed into service to explain why a thief robs a bank or why a man rapes a nine-year-old girl?

Evidence for Reincarnation

So much for the theory; what is the evidence for it?

Here are a few illustrations that serve as proof. In 1951 a boy was born in India who at the age of four began to tell his parents that he actually belonged to a family in the town of Kosi Klan, six miles away. He knew many details of this other family, and when a visit was arranged, he actually recognized them as his parents. He was able to recognize other members of the family and knew intimate details about their lives and existence. Interestingly, they had a son who had died a year before this younger boy had been born. The family concluded that their son had been reborn. Similar accounts have happened in different parts of the world.[5]

Shirley MacLaine has other kinds of evidence that she had previous existences. Through consulting a channeler (a medium), she has been able to speak to entities that tell about her past lives. These have told her who she was and where she lived.

On a plane I sat next to a woman who lived in Pennsylvania but as a child had visions and dreams of another home, in some other part of the country. One day, while on vacation in Vermont, she actually visited the home that had been a part of her inner consciousness. She came to believe that she had lived in that house during the 1800s and actually knew the name of the person she had been previously.

In order to assess the evidence we have to ask: when and where did this theory of death begin? And is there good reason to believe that the preceding data has an alternate, more plausible explanation?

The Origin of Reincarnation

In the last chapter we learned that Satan redefined the meaning of God in the Garden of Eden. There, he also redefined the meaning of death. Though God had said that the man and the woman would die if they ate the forbidden fruit, Satan countered, "You surely shall not die!" (Genesis 3:4) Rather than death, he promised them life.

Just as man was not incredulous enough to assume that he could be God without qualification, so the promise that there would be no death had to be reinterpreted to make it believable. Thus the idea arose that although the body dies, the soul passes on to the next existence without any apparent changes in one's personality; death is to be accepted as the consequence of cyclical time. There is no personal God to whom one must give an account, and so we can delete fearful contemplations about death from our imagination.

Many supposedly reliable studies prove that death is not to be feared. Numerous people, hovering between life and death, have reported experiences that were reassuring and even delightful. Some claim that they were carried away in ecstasy and actually regretted that they had to return to this mundane, earthly existence. Many said they saw light.

Reincarnationism is appealing because it encourages people to continue to live the way they are (most people think they are at least as good as the next person) without having to admit their sin and helplessness before God. At death, God simply does not show up. There is no personal accountability, no judgment. Just the opportunity to go around one more time trying to "get it right."

So in the end, everyone wins. As F. LaGard Smith says in critiquing reincarnation:

So *everybody wins*, including the guy at the office who cheated you out of a promotion, the parent who may have sexually abused you, the spouse who left you for somebody else. That's right, *everybody wins*— even Attila the Hun, Adolf Hitler, Idi Amin, Colonel Gaddafi, and the Ayatollah Khomeini. Granted they may be the last wave, pulling up the rear; but as they come across the finish line, everyone will be waiting there to cheer them on. *With reincarnation, nobody loses!*[6]

The Bible teaches differently, of course. In the end, all those whose names are not written in the Book of Life will stand before God to be judged for every single deed they have ever done. Here is the end of all those who accept the lies of the Antichrist: "And the smoke of their torment goes up forever and ever; and they have no rest day and night, those who worship the beast and his image, and whoever receives the mark of his name" (Revelation 14:11).

Those who follow Satan will be in conscious torment forever and ever. They will be alone with their memories, their regrets, and their guilt. And there will never be another opportunity to go around once more to "get it right."

A Biblical Interpretation

Some New Age writers, including Shirley MacLaine, try to make the Bible teach reincarnation. Let's consider just two of the passages frequently used.

In Matthew 17:11-12, Christ says that Elijah is coming and will restore all things, and then continues, "But I say to you, that Elijah already came, and they did not recognize him, but did to him whatever they wished. So also the Son of Man is going to suffer at their hands."

The disciples understood him to be referring to John the Baptist. So, the argument goes, John was Elijah reincarnated. But there are two reasons to reject this interpretation. First, John expressly denied that he was Elijah (John 1:19-21). Second, at his birth we are told in effect that John's ministry was *reminiscent* of Elijah, "And it is he who will go as a forerunner before him in the spirit and power of Elijah" (Luke 1:17).

Another passage frequently cited by reincarnationists is John 9:1-3, where Jesus responds to a question from the disciples about the origin of a blind man's malady. Was it because of this man's sin or that of his parents that he was born blind? Christ replies, "It was neither that this man sinned, nor his parents; but it was that the works of God might be displayed in him." The New Ager's argument is this: if there was a possibility that this man's illness was the result of his own sin, it must be that he committed it *before* his birth. After all, he was *born* blind.

But the argument fails for two reasons. First, the disciples' question is based on the Jewish notion that sin can be inherited from one's parents. Also it was believed that a baby could sin in the womb. But there is no evidence that the Jews believed in reincarnation. Second, Christ clearly repudiates any kind of belief in reincarnation or karma. The blindness, Christ says, *was not the result of his sin or that of his parents.* So much for reincarnationism.

How then do we account for the evidence for reincarnation? The Bible teaches that there are intelligent spirits in the world called demons (New Agers call them by the neutral term *entities*) who enter into human beings and communicate information to them—information about the past, the present and, in a limited way, even about the future. These spirits take the identity of human beings, often claiming to be some important person from the past. Since these intelligent spirits are well acquainted with other people and places, it is easy for them to communicate these "memories" to the people they inhabit.

Be assured of this: no one ever communicates with the dead. No one has spoken to your dead uncle, grandfather, or mother. No one has ever communicated with Houdini or with so-called "ascended masters." Those who claim such exclusive encounters are either faking it or they are in communication with demons—wicked spirits who delight to deceive. *There is a transmigration of demons, but not a transmigration of souls.*

Reincarnationists willingly admit that they are in contact with spirits, but they believe that these "entities" are guides, who either are the dead or those who can speak to the dead for them. They assume that these spirits speak only the truth and therefore can be fully trusted. Or some New Agers actually believe that they can distinguish the evil spirits from the good ones! The lady with whom I rode on the plane admitted that she was in touch with the spirit world but assured me that she shunned evil spirits and had contact only with the good ones.

"How do you tell the difference?" I asked.

"It's easy. The good ones are always clothed with light."

Read the New Age literature and that word *light* appears again and again. A poster advertising a prophetess who puts people in touch with "ascended masters" reads, "Beyond Channeling—Feel the Incomparable Light." Some who have died and returned claim they have no fear of death because they have seen a "tunnel of light."

So it is. Satan's deception is not new. Paul wrote about this form of *light*. "For such men are false apostles, deceitful workers, disguising themselves as apostles of Christ. And no wonder, for even Satan disguises himself as an angel of light" (2 Corinthians 11:13-14).

These mortals claim they see light and that they have the ability to distinguish the true from the false. But the New Testament says nothing about good entities who can be contacted for information. Indeed, God warns against such occult practices because only demons are available for such an interesting rendezvous.

Since satanic light is a rejection of the true light, the battle is really one between light and darkness. People who would never trust a stranger are receiving information from entities that stand in sharp opposition to the truth of God.

Fortunately, reincarnationism is a lie. Here again we can take the offensive and point out that only Christianity can answer the problem of justice. We can say to those suffering from painful diseases that they are not getting what they deserve; we can tell those who are victims of injustice or accidents that they are not being punished for something they do not remember doing.

What is more, we can say that in the end not everyone will win, for the simple reason that some do not deserve to! The murderer and rapist will not be able to escape personal responsibility. In the end, Stalin will not get off the hook because he eventually reached some nebulous state of perfection.

Yet mercy can be received in this life that enables us to escape the wrath of God. This is not because God is lenient and indifferent to justice. Christ bore the consequences of sin for those who believe in Him. He made it possible for God to "even the score" without sending us to hell forever. "Therefore having been justified by faith, we have peace with God through our Lord Jesus Christ" (Romans 5:1).

So there is still hope for the wicked in this life. Even the murderer or the rapist can take advantage of Christ's payment for sin. But once they forfeit this opportunity, they will not have another chance in the world to come, because the Bible teaches "it is appointed for men to die once and after this comes judgment" (Hebrews 9:27).

Would you rather entrust your eternal soul to an impersonal force called karma that doles out punishment without regard to your circumstances or the disposition of your own heart? Or would you prefer to entrust yourself to a merciful God who sent His Son to bear the penalty for those who believe? Would you prefer to tell those who are suffering that they are getting exactly what they deserve? Or would you like to be able to say to them that Christ's death means that they need not get what they deserve? The supposed advantages of reincarnation fade rapidly when compared to the teaching of Scripture.

The popularity of the New Age Movement gives us a wide-open door to display the compassion of Christ rather than the indifference of a cruel and uncaring law of cause and effect.

The truth is on our side. Let's shout it from the housetops!

Chapter Six

Moral Relativism:
The Third Spiritual Flaw

*B*ehind every worldview there lies the question of morality: how can we distinguish good from evil? What are the standards by which we structure society?

The third spiritual flaw was Satan's attack on moral absolutes. He began by introducing doubt into Eve's mind regarding the clear command of God. "Indeed, has God said?" (Genesis 3:1) Now that the seed of doubt had been planted, he watered it with the allurement of special knowledge. If she and her husband disobeyed, their eyes would be opened and they would be like God, "knowing good and evil" (v. 5).

No need to consult God about moral choices. Adam and Eve could do whatever seemed good based on their own finite reasoning and feeling. They were the masters of their fate, the captains of their souls.

But this promise, like others made by Satan, has proved to be elusive and confusing. Yes, fallen man does have a moral nature that gives him some clue regarding morality;

yes, he does have a mind that he can use to give reasons for his actions. But the bottom line is that without a revelation from God (the Bible), mankind simply does not have an objective basis for morality.

Relativism is the word we use to describe the popular American belief "What is true for me may not be true for you." As far back as 1976 a survey of 9,000 graduate students in 40 universities showed that 51 percent believed in moral relativism. But with the rise of the New Age Movement, we can expect that the slide toward relativism will continue to increase at a faster pace. The reasons why will become clear in a moment.

John Dewey, the philosopher and educator, is credited for giving relativism respectability here in America. He believed that morality, like language, varied from culture to culture and therefore no one moral belief was superior to another. The Eskimos who practice infanticide and women of Tibet who have several husbands are all on the same moral plane. The only principle that should govern behavior is whether or not it works. And what works today may not work tomorrow and what works for me may not work for you.

In the 1960s this theory became known as situationism, the teaching that there could be no objectivity in morals. Morality was determined by whatever the situation called for at the moment. Lying, stealing, and adultery *become* right under certain conditions. We determine when the Ten Commandments apply and when they do not.

Though relativism (or pragmatism) has gained widespread acceptance, such a theory simply cannot be rationally justified. For one thing, if the end justifies the means, as Dewey and the situationists believe, then we must discover some objective end—some goal that is worthy of the means. But such a goal cannot arise from within man himself for he cannot see the end from the beginning. Only God can tell us life's ultimate purpose. Second, such a philosophy has been used to justify the most hideous behavior. If Hitler had a worthy goal for 90 million Germans (he believed he did), he had every right to kill 6 million Jews to accomplish that end.

The general concept that whatever works is right has made serious inroads into the church and has opened the door to the New Age Movement. Some Christians think that because transcendental meditation lowers one's blood pressure, it must be good. After all, it works. But astrology works too and so does acupuncture and hypnotism. A graduate of *est* said, "I don't care how much of this is [bunk]. It's changed my life."[1]

Bunk may not be able to change a person's life, but Satan can. Listen to Christ's words recorded in Matthew 7:21-23:

Not everyone who says to Me, "Lord, Lord," will enter the kingdom of heaven; but he who does the will of My Father who is in heaven. Many will say to Me on that day, "Lord, Lord, did we not prophesy in your Name, and in Your name cast out demons, and in Your name perform many miracles?" And then I will declare to them, "I never knew you; depart from Me, you who practice lawlessness."

Here were people helping other people; they were doing miracles. They had found something that worked. Nevertheless they were barred from the kingdom and were told that they were practicing lawlessness!

The image of the New Age Movement in America is that of a benevolent worldview, interested in the harmony of mankind and peace and justice for all. The techniques used to plug into the spiritual forces of the universe exist solely for the development of man and the exploration of his latent potential. Who can quarrel with such lofty ideals?

But these beautiful platitudes are no different than the seductive tree that Eve could not resist. She did not realize that there is an ugly side to Satan's lofty appeal. Just so, behind the mask of peace and love, there lies the complete destruction of morality. The New Age Movement represents a much more serious attack on morality than the pragmatism of Dewey. Because of its presuppositions, it cannot, strictly speaking, make any distinctions between good and evil at all. Of necessity, it is the most cruel and barbaric worldview that one can imagine. Logically, Hinduism cannot even say that Hitler and Stalin were evil!

To understand why the New Age Movement is devoid of a moral foundation, we must review a bit of philosophical background. After all, ideas have consequences. Once we begin with certain premises, we must follow them wherever they lead.

God Is Everything

Pantheism, you will recall, is the belief that God is all and all is God. Because all that exists is God, pantheism of necessity holds that God is both evil and good. Previously we referred to Allan Watts as saying that life is like a play where we see both evil and good on the stage, but behind the platform they are friends. Behind the curtain God and Satan go hand in hand. Indeed, God and Satan should not be distinguished because they are but aspects of the Great One, the force that unites all things. *Everything* is God; therefore He is both evil and good.

But the matter doesn't end there. Remember that for the pantheist, the final reality of the universe is spiritual, not material. In fact, the material world is a hindrance to our becoming one with the infinite force, the cosmic energy called God. Strictly speaking, matter is an illusion, and so is the supposed conflict between right and wrong. Only the uninformed make such distinctions. As Yen-Men, one of the great Eastern teachers, said: the conflict between right and wrong is the sickness of the mind.

The goal of pantheism is for the individual to lose himself or herself in the "eternal nothingness of God." Life is a dream and someday we will awake to realize that we were dreaming. That awakening will be a loss of consciousness as we are united with the eternal, unknowable force. To speak of good and evil as opposites is to betray the fact that we are still tied to the elementary distinctions of physical existence. In self-realization, claim New Agers, we get beyond such distinctions.

This is why guru Bhagwan Shree Rajneesh states, "I don't believe in morality . . . and I am bent on destroying it."[2] Again he says that his community "makes no difference between the demonic and the divine."[3]

Swami Vivekananda says, "Good and evil are one and the same."[4] He goes on to say that the murderer too is God.

Os Guiness articulates the moral dilemma for the pantheist who must, of necessity, be indifferent to distinctions between good and evil.

Thus the ideal is to attain to the level of bliss where one is so transcendent in consciousness that he is beyond the distinctions of good and evil! This has given rise to the bizarre idea that a true test would be to do some deed of total evil and then check to see if there is any pang of feeling or remorse.[5]

Perhaps now we can better understand the exchange that took place between TV talk-show host Oprah Winfrey and self-proclaimed satanist Michael Aquino. On the February 17, 1988 program, he described satanists as "very decent, very law-abiding people . . . [who] have nothing to do with evil."[6] Oprah was surprised that this was the case, given the gruesome stories connected with satanism that occasionally surface in the news. But Aquino said that the idea that Satan was evil was a gross misconception that he would "lay at the doorstep of the Christian value system."

Indeed! Aquino was right on two counts. First, given the Eastern mindset, satanism is not wrong—precisely because *nothing can be wrong*. There is no distinction between good and evil. The Prophet Isaiah, writing to those who were steeped in the occultism of the day, pronounced, "Woe to those who call evil good, and good evil; who substitute darkness for light and light for darkness; who substitute bitter for sweet, and sweet for bitter!" (Isaiah 5:20)

Second, Aquino blames Christianity for making moral distinctions; it calls satanism evil, for example. That also is true. The Judeo-Christian worldview can call something evil precisely because it does not believe that everything is God; nor does it teach that individuals are God and therefore have the right to do as they please.

John Upland, who became an avid disciple of the Indian guru Bhagwan Shree Rajneesh for approximately seven months, said, "Rajneesh gives you the opportunity to sin like you've never sinned before. Only he doesn't call it sin. 'The path to desirelessness is through desire.' "[7] So the path to moral restraint is rampant indulgence.

Just recently a story surfaced about a teenage girl who was missing for several months. Because the police appeared to have no leads, the parents hired a private detective to investigate the case. After a month, he discovered that she had been murdered as a sacrifice by a satanic cult. But he refused to give more details for fear of retaliation. It turned out that the police also knew the details but would not prosecute for the same reason.

Such a gruesome story seems to be contrary to the promises of love and justice that are promoted by the New Agers. But in a pantheistic world, there is no morality. Many decent people who have been lured into the movement have no idea of the consequences of believing that we are all a part of the force. Cruelty and pain are on an equal par with kindness and pleasure.

We Are God

There is another piece to the moral puzzle. As repeatedly emphasized, the New Age Movement teaches that we are all God. Therefore we are in charge of our own destiny. If evil befalls us, it is actually because *we choose it!* This is

what Shirley MacLaine teaches in her seminars. Consciously or unconsciously, we choose whatever happens.

A graduate of *est* (Erhard Seminar Training) stated that
she listened for two hours while two women therapists
explained how the Jews must have wanted to be burned by
the Germans, and that those who starve in the Sahara
Desert must want it to happen. When asked what can be
done about a child starving in the desert, one of the therapists snapped angrily, "What can I do if a child is determined to starve?"[8]

Let's hear it from Erhard himself: "As you can see, this
universe is perfect. Don't lie about it. You're God in your
universe. You caused it. You pretended not to cause it so
you could play in it."[9]

The result is that I need never feel guilty for the way I
treat you. Even betrayal, theft, or personal injury need not
fill me with regret. There are reasons why this happened,
reasons that absolve me from remorse. No need to apolo-
gize in a perfect universe.

Terry Cole-Whittaker says that guilt is usually accompa-
nied by or preceded by "a false sense of responsibility for
someone else. Both guilt and responsibility for someone
else are a lie."[10] If you have a sexual relationship with
someone that resulted in hurt feelings, you should not feel
guilty. That person needed the experience to develop his
own godhood, and since he is in control of his own destiny,
you should not regret the part you played in his emotional
trauma.

Let's review the logic:

First, I am as much a part of God as you are. The distinctions between good and evil are illusionary; they are nothing more than the sickness of the mind.

Second, as God, we are totally in charge of ourselves and
determine our own fate. You choose to have me hit you,
steal your wife, or vandalize your car.

Third, whatever happens is but the outworking of justice—our karma has decreed our fate. This explains why

one person is born deformed, why another is permanently disabled in an auto accident, or why you were abused by your father.

No use shedding tears; there can be neither regret nor remorse in a world where good and evil are illusionary, in a world where we have chosen our fate and in which we get our just desserts. Everything is perfectly and delicately balanced.

This explains why Ghandi, so admired by Americans because of the favorable publicity he received in the movie that bears his name, was morally insensitive to the murder of the Jews during World War II. Even after the full extent of the Holocaust was revealed, he told one of his biographers that "the Jews would have died anyway . . . so they might just as well have died significantly."

Perhaps now we are in a better position to understand why Hindus consider evil to be illusionary. This seems to soften the harsh reality of saying that God is both evil and good. Rather than facing the distortions of pantheism, it seems more acceptable to say that evil really does not exist at all. Mind you, this assertion does not lessen the pain of those who are starving, nor does it heal the emotional hurt of rejection experienced by those who are on the lower rungs of the caste system.

Space forbids a detailed analysis of the moral inconsistencies of pantheism. Because all men are created in the image of God, it is impossible to live without moral values. Regardless of what men say about the illusionary character of evil, no one can live that way. That's why the New Age Movement in America continues to talk about morality. Indeed, it appeals to some noble ideals. Adherents assure us they are working for the betterment of the human race. Such claims, of course, are in direct contradiction with the philosophical base of New Age thought.

But speak of a better world they do. Let's look at some of the guidelines that some believe should be used to bring in the New Era.

Rewriting the Ten Commandments

One of the characteristics of Eastern thought is that it is consciously irrational. You cannot lose your identity with the Ultimate Reality if you insist on rationality. Indeed, in mystical experience, one must discard such notions. In the higher realm of reality everything blends into the horizon of infinite spiritual existence.

Yet, as already mentioned, the New Agers have a morality anyway. Though distinctions between right and wrong are but the sickness of the mind, at least some adherents believe that moral guidelines are important. Possibly the New Agers can justify this inconsistency by saying that moral judgments are necessary for those who have not yet reached enlightenment.

Whatever the rationale, the fact is that the New Agers have their own 10 commandments engraved in stone near Elberton, Georgia. The story goes that a man named Robert C. Christian came to a farm there and asked the proprietor if he would undertake construction of a massive granite monument which would list 10 guiding principles for all to see. Apparently tourists worldwide come to visit the site, which has many occult associations.

The message on the stones is in eight modern languages and four dead languages. The sponsors say that these are the 10 guides for the New Age of Reason. A spokesman for the group gives this explanation:

> It is very probable that humanity now possesses the knowledge needed to establish effective world government. In some way that knowledge must be widely seeded in the consciousness of all mankind.
>
> Very soon the hearts of our human family must be touched and warmed so we will welcome a global rule of reason. . . . The approaching crisis may make mankind willing to accept a system of world law . . . with such a system we could eliminate war. . . . There are alternatives to Armageddon.[12]

The commandments themselves speak of the need to reduce the population of the earth to one-half billion, down from the present estimate of 4.8 billion. The people who remain should be protected with fair laws and just courts; there would also be a world court to resolve international disputes. The inscription ends by speaking about the need for truth, beauty, love, and harmony. And finally, we are admonished to leave room for nature.

It is difficult to know how seriously we should regard these guidelines. But the fact that their origin is shrouded in mystery and that they have as their focus a one-world government should alert us to the fact that they have more than incidental significance.

At any rate, notice the strategy. Those who desire to see the world ruled by a single government appeal to legitimate areas of concern—the environment, starvation, and the threat of war. Second, they clothe their aims in lofty platitudes that make criticism difficult. Who can argue against justice, love, and tolerance?

But Satan and his followers have no plans to be tolerant. As we shall see in a future chapter, they have an agenda they plan to follow to bring about world government. And this means that they must strongly oppose those who stand in their way. Indeed, New Age literature speaks openly about the need to purify the earth of dissenters. In the book *Prophecies and Predictions*, author Moira Timms says that "the plagues of Revelation are special packages of karma visited upon the obstinate that they might awaken to their wrong attitudes . . . animals that don't adapt become extinct."[13] Those who won't "get with the program" will be dealt with harshly.

The Bible predicts that Antichrist will force people to fall in line with his agenda. Those who refuse to take his mark will be ostracized, tortured, and killed. "And he causes all, the great and the small, the rich and the poor, and the free men and the slaves, to be given a mark on their right hand, or on their forehead, and he provides that no one should be able to buy or to sell, except the one who has the mark, either the name of the beast or the number of his name" (Revelation 13:16-17).

During those days people will either choose to worship the beast or be put to death. The worship of the true Christ will be a crime. Those who refuse the coming transformation will be considered irreconcilable outcasts.

The bottom line is that the New Agers do have a morality after all. Although pantheism leads logically to the destruction of all morality, mankind cannot tolerate the obliteration of his conscience. In the final analysis, the New Agers revert back to the old pragmatic notion that the end justifies the means. The end in this case is the New World Order and the means will be to eradicate any opposition to the Grand Plan.

Thus Satan's lie that man can distinguish good from evil without divine help will bring about the eventual destruction of society as we know it. In place of God's morality, man will choose his own goals and values and the means to achieve them. For those who fall under the hand of this regime, morality will not be an illusion but a painful reality.

Esotericism:
The Fourth Spiritual Flaw

Listen to the Great Invocation of the New Age:

From the point of Light within the Mind of God
Let light stream forth into the minds of men
Let Light descend on Earth

From the point of Love within the Heart of God
Let love stream forth into the hearts of men
May Christ return to earth

From the center where the Will of God is known
Let purpose guide the little wills of men
The purpose which the Masters know and serve

From the center which we call the race of men
Let the Plan of Love and Light work out
And may it seal the door where evil dwells

Let Light and Love and Power restore the Plan on
Earth[1]

This invocation is used daily by those who are trying to work with one another and with God in bringing peace to earth. But the God referred to is the pantheistic god; the Christ is Maitreya; and the Light is that of the enlightened mind. Interestingly, according to the survey done by Andrew Greeley, 5 percent of Americans claim they have already been "bathed in light."[2] They have had an esoteric experience, a personal encounter that has given them special knowledge.

When Satan came to Adam and Eve, he persuaded them to make their own decisions without consulting God. To do this, the man and the woman had to learn to trust their own intuitions rather than obey a clear command. In return, their eyes would be opened, and they would experience enlightenment. The scheme worked. "When the woman saw that the tree was good for food, and that it was a delight to the eyes, and that the tree was desirable to make one wise, she took from its fruit and ate; and she gave also to her husband with her, and he ate" (Genesis 3:6).

The fruit was appealing and looked harmless to the woman. Her own enlightenment would be a more reliable guide to reality than the bare command of God. Through personal observation she could tell that God was being unfair. What she touched, tasted, and smelled became her guide to reality. Feeling was more important than thinking. With her own eyes opened, she would no longer have to depend on God's guidance.

Satan's ultimate desire is not for men and women to commit immorality or even to look to astrology for guidance or to be healed by crystals. All these techniques of the New Age Movement are but stepping-stones to his most subtle deception, namely, *the duplication of religious experience.*

All the roads lead to this one: *Satan wants humans to encounter him and think they are in touch with the living God.* The bottom line is that he wants to give his followers a "satanic conversion." To duplicate a divine encounter is the height of his rebellion. When he fell he said he would be "like the Most High" (Isaiah 14:14). He thinks this miracle is proof that he is succeeding! To effect a spiritual conversion is his most dazzling deception!

That's why Satan makes the same claims as Christ. "I am the light of the world," Christ asserted (John 8:12; 9:5). Satan responds by advertising his own brand of light. Indeed, New Age Movement literature is filled with references to "light" or "enlightenment." In her seminars Shirley MacLaine tells people about the watching bubble of white light that is revealing a part of God within them which they have not yet recognized. This light is assuredly a shroud for the darkness that will eventually come to all of Satan's followers.

Again Christ promised special knowledge to those who believe on Him: "And this is eternal life, that they may know Thee, the only true God, and Jesus Christ whom Thou hast sent" (John 17:3). True to form, Satan promises that his followers can receive a special initiation, a "transformation of consciousness" that makes them members of an elite group.

Here again the New Age turns out to be a revival of the Old Age, for the teaching of the "mystery religions" during the pagan days of Greece and Rome was based on the idea that there was secret knowledge that could be obtained by searching the depths of one's own soul. Through mystical encounters with cosmic powers, enlightenment was possible.

Marilyn Ferguson says that if we want to have a new perception of reality, "the first step is an entry point . . . a mystical psychic experience."[3]

Let's pause here for a moment of analysis. The entry point is a spiritual experience, but what is a spiritual experience? Though Ferguson does not define it, of necessity it must be *an encounter with another spiritual being.* But there is more than one spiritual being in the universe. God, angels, demons, and humans all have spiritual capacities.

How can one know which spirit has been contacted?

Since a person cannot have a spiritual experience with himself, it follows that the New Agers must be making contact with some other spiritual beings. Good angels are off-limits because they respond primarily to God and minister only to those who are children of God through faith in Jesus Christ. Nowhere does the Bible teach that we should make contact with these beings; rather, it forbids contacting any supernatural power except God.

So either the New Agers are making contact with the true God or wicked spirits who are available for communication. God must be ruled out, since the New Agers (1) deny that He has an existence independent of the universe, and (2) reject the belief that Christ is the only way to God the Father. That leaves demonic spirits who are only too glad to make contact with humans and give them a genuine "spiritual experience."

C.S. Lewis perceptively realized that the highest form of deception would be for demons to duplicate spiritual experiences. The fictional demon Screwtape, in giving instructions to his underling Wormwood, says, "I have great hopes that we shall learn in due time how to emotionalize and mythologize their science to such an extent that what is, in effect, a belief in us, (though not under that name) will creep in while the human mind remains closed to belief in the Enemy [God]."[4]

Secular humanism has built a wall of reason around the human mind, insulating many from belief in the true God. Now, in the next stage of man's decline, Satan and his demons penetrate this prison of reason, offering a fulfillment which secularism lacks. Always disguising themselves, they blend "spiritual experience" with science, nutrition, the environmental movement, medicine, yoga, hypnotism, and a host of other Eastern teachings. Beginning with small steps, they lead individuals down the path to altered states of consciousness, so that their devilish control can be strengthened.

Think of the sinister delight Satan has when taking the place of God in the life of an individual, even to the point of granting his client a spiritual conversion! This explains why those who have had this initiation are so convinced they alone have the right perception of reality. They think they are plugged into the energy of the universe and have been reconciled to a pantheistic god who is indeed all there is. How can they be so sure? They've experienced it!

The Bible teaches that the earth is populated with spirit beings called demons who are only too happy to communicate information and become a person's guide. Many people falsely believe that demons communicate only evil ideas, not realizing that these spirits may often give good advice and even mouth sound doctrine. When our Lord was on earth, demons frequently confessed that He was the Christ. Interestingly, when a demon-possessed slave girl followed Paul around the city of Philippi, she kept saying, "These men are bond-servants of the Most High God, who are proclaiming to you the way of salvation" (Acts 16:17). Her "spirit of divination," as the Bible calls it, was meticulously correct in its assessment. Yet a few days later, Paul cast the spirit from the girl.

Demons are liars who receive perverted satisfaction from deceiving gullible humans. When the truth serves their purposes, they will use it; when half-truths are called for, they have them in their arsenal; but lying is their most popular weapon. They are assigned to a certain individual and, because they study the behavior and history of their subject, they become very knowledgeable regarding his or her past. After the person has died, these spirits are open to the possibility of communicating with relatives and friends who want to have a conversation with their departed loved one. A channeler is contacted who purports to "call up" the dead and establish communication. But in fact, the communication is not with the dead, but with demons who impersonate the dead.

Satan is the leader of these multiplied millions of demons. That's why counterfeit conversions can take place anywhere, anytime. How does one enter into this esoteric encounter, the experience of enlightenment? There are many paths that lead to the demonic kingdom.

The Doorway of Meditation

In her book *The Aquarian Conspiracy*, Marilyn Ferguson says that a "paradigm shift" is taking place in the West. We are leaving the world of logic and reason and are appealing to the world of imagination and feeling. We are going from the "left brain" to the "right brain."

What is the result of this?

"We are not victims or pawns . . . we control,"[5] she writes. We now are left in charge of ourselves. The spiritual experiences we have are so awesome, we have the feeling that we are in complete control.

These experiences, she writes, assure us that there is no such thing as sin. "Human nature is neither bad nor good."

"Only religion can carry the load," she says, but she is quick to point out that it is "not the religion of the churches but the spiritual dimension that transcends customs and politics."

How can one have such a spiritual experience? Ferguson says it comes by emptying the mind of all conscious thought by means of meditation. She says that psychedelic drugs speed up the process. Both lead to the emptying of the mind and the immobilization of the will.[6]

On the surface, practices such as transcendental meditation appear to be harmless and, in the minds of millions of Americans, actually beneficial to the mind and body. What could possibly be wrong with spending time trying to empty your mind of all of the pressures of life and just think about *nothing?* Combine that with exercises that demand incredible concentration and your blood pressure is sure to drop and your finely tuned body will feel much better.

But this teaching is based on some heavy religious commitments. First, there is the pantheistic belief that we must unite the soul with the one unified force of the universe. There is, after all, only one continuous reality and everything is connected to everything else.

Second, there is the assumption that rationality is actually a hindrance to this oneness and mystical unity with God. As long as I am thinking about *something*, I perceive myself to be distinct from the objects of this world. So I must have an experience in which such distinctions disappear, that I might lose my identity like a drop of water in the vast ocean of impersonal energy. To achieve this, *I must destroy the mind.*

If you think we have overstated the case, let's catch up on a bit of philosophical background and get some perspective. Remember that the Eastern religions teach that in the beginning the universe was a unity; there was but one substance, one all-encompassing reality. Then through a mysterious process this unity was shattered; there was not only mind but also matter—and matter itself has many different levels of reality. There are rocks, but also plants, then animals, and finally, man. Our problem is that our minds tend to think about these objects—but it is precisely such thinking that keeps us at the lower levels of experience. *If we could do away with such specific thoughts and concentrate only on the one general, contentless reality, we would be in harmony with God.* The goal of meditation, then, is to empty the mind of all specific ideas so that an ultimate experience of unity might be achieved.

Two consequences follow. First, the Easterner can truly say that what a man believes is not important. Indeed, it were best if we had no beliefs—all such specific ideas shut us off from ultimate reality. As someone has said, "A man is considered to be a Hindu in good standing not by what he believes but by what he does." At this point there are, of course, some inconsistencies—Easterners do give lectures, write books, and hold seminars. But this is only to get people going in the right direction. After they have embarked on their journey, their previous religious beliefs fall away like leaves from a dead tree. So you can believe whatever you like, but eventually if you follow the lead of the guru, you will soon get beyond doctrinal beliefs.

This explains why we are told that transcendental meditation can be harmonized with all religions including Christianity. Potential converts are told that they need not discard the past, just "transcend" it. This sounds appealing to the pluralistic American mind.

Second, we must break down the natural resistance we have to an invasion of some foreign power. We must surrender our wills by emptying the mind. When we concentrate on a poem or solving a problem, we focus on various associations of images and thoughts. Since such thinking is a barrier to unity with the one all-inclusive reality, the ultimate goal of meditation is the destruction of human rationality.

In his discussion of Hindu mysticism, S.N. Dasgupta gives us the necessary stages for "self-realization." Yoga, he says, "aims solely to stop the movement of mind and to prevent its natural tendency towards comparison, classification, association, assimilation, and the like."[7] There is then the transformation of the mind, where the entire subject-object distinction disappears. This is an experience that is beyond rational discussion and thought. The mind no longer thinks of anything, but is absorbed with the One Reality.

This technique is known as the *mantra* used by Buddhists, Hindus, and Muslims. This meditation utilizes repetition of a word or phrase to condition the mental state of the participant. Such repetition produces an altered state of consciousness which leads to the mystical oneness with God or Ultimate Reality. What is important is that the word or phrase be stripped of meaning so that it will not lead to a particular thought or association of ideas. The goal is the suppression of all thought.

At this point, the mind has miraculous powers over natural objects and receives special revelations. Yet even so, says Dasgupta, it has not attained its ultimate goal. Now the yogi "steadily proceeds toward that ultimate stage in which his mind will be disintegrated and his self will shine forth in its own light and he himself will be absolutely free in bondless, companionless loneliness of self-illumination."[8]

Dasgupta concludes, "The destruction of the mind, of course, also involves the ultimate destruction of this intuition itself. So neither this intuition nor our ordinary logical thought is able to lead us ultimately to self-realization."[9]

This conversion experience does not come easily. TM involves strenuous bodily exercises and hours of mind-control practice. At first the yogi gains full control over all voluntary muscles through various breathing exercises and by practicing precise bodily positions. Within time he progresses to gain control even of *in*voluntary muscles, including the heart and stomach. All of this preparation is to help his quest for final self-realization so that the chance of external bodily disturbances and internal disturbances due to passions and the like have been minimized. Having attained such self-mastery, the destruction of rational thought, which is the ultimate goal of yoga, becomes a possibility.[10]

And how can such a state be maintained? Normal reasoning must be permanently displaced as the means of comprehending reality. There must be the settled conviction that ultimate reality is unrecognizable to the human mind. TM acts as a conditioning process which substitutes mystical experience for the *logos* or the reasoning powers of the mind. This state, often called that of "pure consciousness," causes the individual to go *beyond* personality, *beyond* morality, and *beyond* knowledge. Satan's conversion experience is complete—the transformation of consciousness has occurred. There is only abstract unity, a state that approaches total oblivion.

Enlightenment, we are told, has at last been achieved. The individual, at last, is at rest. He has been bathed in light. But we may ask: at what price? The entire human personality has been practically extinguished.

The Doorway of Drugs

The process we have described can be wearisome. Drugs enable seekers to take a shortcut. Marilyn Ferguson says that the psychedelic experience is a faster route to a new perception of reality. In Annette Hollander's book *How to Help Your Child Have a Spiritual Life*, she gives the account of many people who have had such mystical encounters. Many tell of how they had to reject reason and logical thought. One writes, "I had two very heavy spiritual experiences while on LSD at the ages of 26 and 28. I was having a conversation with something that wasn't very visible, tangible, material. . . . Lasting influence? Definitely . . . it's the window of the house that I'm living in."[11]

The experiences that people report in altered states of consciousness as a result of LSD and other psychedelic drugs are identical to the experiences reported by Hindu gurus in the depths of meditation or yoga. That's why Timothy Leary says drugs have become the sacraments of the New Age.

As Christians, we know that the passive mental states associated with transcendental meditation and drugs open the personality to demonic activity. Even Eastern gurus frequently warn about the dangers of demonic possession and the madness that might accompany such an experience. Mediums, seeking to call up the dead (actually evil spirits as previously explained), try to experience an altered state of consciousness so that they can make contact with the regions beyond.

There are other routes to a spiritual experience, including music and hypnotism. Think of walking down a hallway that has many doors. You can choose anyone that appeals to you and find that you are entering the same room as your friend who took another door. Conversion can take place in many ways.

The Frightful Deception

Read Shirley MacLaine or David Spangler or dozens of other New Age enthusiasts, and you will soon learn that they see themselves as perfectly capable of interpreting the world of spiritual entities, out-of-body experiences, and visions of light. Like Eve who was mesmerized by the beauty of the tree, these individuals are convinced that they have nothing to fear as they venture into the spirit world to encounter it for themselves. Intuition and experience are sufficient guides to reality.

But is any one of us in a position to interpret such experiences correctly? The answer is no. All human experience is finite; we all are open to numerous deceptions. Like an ant crawling out from the crack of a rock, we cannot see the whole world, nor can we peer very far into the future—we're not in a position to make ultimate judgments.

Elizabeth Kubler-Ross, whose book entitled *On Death and Dying* propelled her to the forefront of studies on the terminally ill, has since become involved with psychic phenomena. She has conversations with spirit beings who visit her quite regularly; some she numbers among her friends. Through her studies of those who have died and then been resuscitated, she has concluded that death need be feared by no one. In the twilight zone between life and death people tell of visions of a benevolent Christ who welcomes everyone into heaven. Many claim to see visions of light that give them a sense of peace and positive expectations.

What we really need is an authority who knows the end from the beginning—we need to receive our information from God Himself who is acquainted with the eventual destiny of all mankind. Only someone with such knowledge (I speak of omniscience) is qualified to tell us about the spirit world and what lies on the other side of death.

Consider the modern channeler who has conversations with "entities," or "ascended masters," believed to be the spirits of departed humans who have paid all of their karmic debts. Shirley MacLaine shares the stories she has heard about herself and others through a channeler called Kevin, who contacts entities that lived on the earth thousands of years ago. Another movie star, Linda Evans, is reportedly in contact with a channeler who speaks to Ramtha, an all-wise 35,000-year-old spirit. According to a friend, Linda "believes everything Ramtha tells her, including where she should live and what investments she should make."[12] But how does she know that these masters are indeed telling her the truth? She is but one person in a vast universe populated by good spirits and bad. Might she not be deceived?

The famous spiritist Emanuel Swedenborg realized that the spirits he associated with were cunning and deceitful. He cautioned:

> When spirits begin to speak with a man, he ought to beware that he believes nothing whatever from them; for they say almost anything . . . they would tell so many lies and indeed with solemn affirmation that a man would be astonished . . . if a man listens and believes they press on, and deceive, and seduce in [many] ways.[13]

Unfortunately, Swedenborg believed his gift of working with spirits was God-given, thus proving that spirits were even more deceptive than he had imagined. Though he recognized they could not be trusted, they convinced him that God had permitted him to work with them.

Such illustrations—and dozens of others might be given—point to the great need for us to have a source whereby information from the spirit world might be interpreted. That source is the Bible, in which God has spoken with clarity and power.

The High Cost of Deception
What are the results of prolonged contact with the demonic kingdom? What happens to those who repeatedly experi-

ence a "transformation of consciousness"? The initial experiences may appear to be positive, but afterward there are negative repercussions, which include:[14]

1. *Dehabilitation.* Work production decreases; the ability to concentrate begins to wane. The long-term results of TM, for example, show a marked decrease in productivity by the fifth year.

2. *Withdrawal.* The person in contact with demonic powers begins to isolate himself from other persons. Rather than increasing the ability to love and reach out to others, he or she becomes more self-absorbed, seeking higher spiritual experiences. The end result is isolation, a preoccupation with the next spiritual high. Perhaps this is what hell is all about—the eternal isolation and absorption of self, which seems enjoyable for the moment.

3. *Depression.* Those who pursue spiritual experiences discover, just as alcoholics do, that the highs become fewer while the lows become deeper. More stimulation is constantly needed to keep the individual functional.

4. *Destruction.* The final state of all who surrender to demonic control, under the guise of self-sufficiency, is eternal hell prepared for the devil and his angels.

When Adam and Eve chose to be guided by self-enlightenment, they elevated themselves above the Almighty. Sweet feelings, magnified by the sensations of the body and soul, became their guide. But it didn't end there. This act that dethroned God's command in favor of their own understanding was later taken a step further. The attempted destruction of God's Word eventually led to the attempted destruction of the human mind in quest of the "ultimate spiritual experience."

Satan, the infamous imitator, has his own conversion experience to give to the unwary as he seeks to enlist men and women into his kingdom. He moves beyond the hedonism of sensual pleasure to the ecstasy of the soul. This brings a loyalty on the part of his subjects that accelerates their final destruction.

As Christians, all the advantages are again on our side. Conversion to Christ takes away our guilt and brings us peace with God. It does this without destroying our rationality or personality. Furthermore, it enables us to find answers to ultimate questions from a trustworthy source. We are not left to our own deceptive desires, but can learn from an ascended Christ who proved His indisputable power over nature and death. There are no negative side effects.

On a talk show, Shirley MacLaine ended her promotion for Hinduism by asking, "What have you got to lose?"

The answer is: "Your eternal soul."

Chapter Eight

Infiltrating the Church

Legend says that the Greeks laid siege to the city of Troy for 10 years but were unable to capture it. In exasperation, a man by the name of Ulysses decided to have a large wooden horse built and left outside the city walls. Then the Greeks sailed away in apparent defeat.

The curious Trojans felt confident enough to drag the horse inside the walls, though a priest named Laocoon warned them not to. He said, "I fear the Greeks, even when bringing gifts." That night Greek soldiers crept out of the horse, opened the city gates, and let the rest of the Greek forces into Troy. The Greeks massacred the people of Troy, and looted and burned the city.

Throughout its 2,000-year history, the church has always been tempted to embrace the disguised enemies in her midst. When Constantine became emperor of the Roman Empire the persecution of the church ended and Christianity became popular. But along with this new acceptance, the church also absorbed the paganism of the day. The

Romans were polytheists who had a god for hunting, a god for buying and selling, a god to protect them on a journey. Rather than standing against such superstitions, the church assigned these responsibilities to dead saints. Thus in violation of Scripture, people would pray to one saint or another depending on the kind of request that was made.

In the 18th century, rationalism arose in Europe. The Enlightenment taught that man could, through the proper use of his own mind, solve all of his problems. God, it was believed, did not interfere in the affairs of men. At best, He created the world and then let it run by itself. Thus the miracles of the Bible were denied. Whereas before unbelievers were generally found only within the world, they now also were found within the church. Theological liberalism was born and became fashionable in thousands of churches in Europe and America.

Today the world is seeping into the church in many ways. We could mention the erosion of moral values, the acceptance of divorce as an answer to marital conflict, and the selfish pursuit of money and status. But the world is also making overtures through the lure of the New Age.

Liberal theologians are of course ready to join hands with the channelers and the astrologers of this age, believing that spiritual experiences are of equal value. The Reverend Gene Seely, an ordained United Methodist minister, says he is quite ready to climb out on a limb with Shirley MacLaine—at least most of the way. One cannot watch her growth, he says, without recalling the parable of Christ about the new wine in old wineskins. Only stretchable wineskins can accommodate the ferment of new truth.

The minister says we must allow for the fact that God may be revealing Himself through experiences such as that of the famous actress. After all, he asks, "How then is the church to deal with such things as reincarnation, trance channeling, out-of-body experiences, clairvoyance, extraterrestrials, telepathy, intelligent energy fields, and nonphysical entities?"[1]

The Spirit, says Seely, works where and when He will. "There is much we do not know as yet. But some things are becoming clear. We are in the time of the greatest spiritual awakening the world has ever known."[2]

Finally, he asks whether indeed it might be that Christ's claims to deity are in fact the *pattern* for every person. "Could it be that we are not sinful at the core of our being after all, but divine? Are you and I really 'gods in the making,' each of us to be realized when we become one with the Father within?"[3]

So there you have it. An ordained Christian minister saying that, yes, Christ was right about His deity, but He is simply the pattern for us all! Shirley MacLaine is right when she says, "I am God!"

Fortunately, such heresy is not yet found within the believing church. But Satan is not content to have theological liberals in his column. He would like to include some who do indeed know God through Christ. Even if he cannot have them forever, he would like to dazzle them with his power.

"For false Christs and false prophets will arise and will show great signs and wonders, so as to mislead, if possible, even the elect" (Matthew 24:24). Those who think that everything that is miraculous is of God will be grievously misled. Unbelievers will rush headlong into the darkness of Satan's power; even believers will be confused and dangerously close to buying into the New Age agenda.

Satan is making a worldwide effort to convert millions to join his army in a futile effort to dethrone God. Think of his daring plan—to find allies within the church that is called to represent Christ who already conquered him on Calvary!

If Satan walked down the aisle of an evangelical church and made a forthright plea for recruits, his sales presentation would be ridiculed and he would be hurriedly excommunicated. So he must think of more subtle ways of marketing his ideas for the Christian community.

The devil seeks to build bridges to the church by using

various deceptions to lure God's sheep into forbidden pathways. To be effective, he knows that his overtures must meet two requirements. They must appear to be biblical, and they must work. Anything less and the evangelical community will not accept them.

Satan therefore markets his ideas through legitimate areas of research and interest. His goal is to introduce some basic misconceptions about Christianity into the minds of believers. Thus, bit by bit, the authority of the Almighty is undermined. When he has found a crack, he keeps pushing until whole multitudes are engulfed at various levels of deception.

Here are some bridges used to introduce New Age ideas into the mainstream of Christian thought.

The Bridge of Psychology

Much of contemporary psychology is built on secular presuppositions; therefore we should not be surprised that both the analysis of man's problems as well as the proposed solutions are tainted with error. Paul Vitz, a professor of psychology at New York University has written, "Psychology as religion exists . . . in great strength throughout the United States . . . [it] is deeply antichristian . . . [yet] it is extensively supported by schools, universities, and social programs financed by taxes collected from Christians."[4]

The premises of secular psychology are: (1) man is a product of blind evolutionary forces and therefore neither "fell into sin" nor must be "redeemed." Then, (2) he has the resources to solve his own problems through education and human effort. And (3) he must come to accept himself just as he is; he must learn to love himself despite his perceived failures.

The basic premise is that of the New Age Movement: *man is his own god and must therefore act accordingly.* Carl Jung in his book *Answers to Job*[5] suggests that God is actually inferior to man and He would like to become man on a permanent basis! Eric Fromm wrote a book whose title was taken directly from the words of Satan—*You Shall Be As Gods.*[6] Thus long before most of us heard of the New Age Movement, secular psychology was already promoting the deity of man.

This explains why so much of contemporary psychology is drifting further off into New Age philosophies and techniques. For some it is yoga with its belief in "self-realization," the belief that one can look within and discover godhood. Others find results by using Silva Mind Control methods. Once again, psychologists are open to whatever works best for each individual. And the techniques of Hinduism seem to rank near the top of the list.

New Age thought penetrates Christianity through its teachings of the "self-concept." With a subtle twist, this expression can be interpreted in such a way as to make it appear as if psychology and Christianity are actually saying the same thing. After all, both disciplines are interested in the way we perceive ourselves.

William Kilpatrick in his book *Psychological Seduction* guides us through the thicket as we try to untangle Christianity from psychology. Kilpatrick, who himself is an associate professor of educational psychology at Boston College, says that psychology is actually a wolf in sheep's clothing; it masquerades as a handmaiden of Christianity but actually seeks to destroy it. That's a harsh judgment of psychology, but Kilpatrick makes his point stick with numerous examples and convincing arguments.

Take, for example, the question: should I love myself? The popular conception is that both Christianity and psychology answer yes; we all ought to love ourselves. Secular psychology teaches that: (1) we should love ourselves despite our faults and sins; indeed if you are sleeping with numerous lovers and you feel guilty about it, you need not change your behavior, but rather you must change your self-concept so that it will embrace your lifestyle. In other words, you have innate worth and can therefore accept yourself unconditionally, *regardless*. Then (2) it teaches that we do not need redemption, but merely enlightenment as to who we really are. All people have within themselves the resources needed to cope with all the problems of life.

Psychology, as Kilpatrick says, has great optimism about raw human nature. All that we need to do to find wholeness is to be ourselves. Indeed, many of our problems, we are told, come about because we think ill of ourselves. The teaching that we are sinners damages our self-concept and therefore lies at the root of many of our emotional ills.

Is this biblical? Kilpatrick correctly observes that this idea of self-worth "is about as far from the gospel as you can travel. Our Lord's greatest wrath was not directed to obvious sinners like Mary Magdalene but at those who were convinced of their own worth."[7]

No biblical saint who met God ever ended up accepting himself unconditionally. Isaiah, in the presence of God, said, "Woe is me, for I am ruined!" (Isaiah 6:5) Job said, "I have heard of Thee by the hearing of the ear; but now my eye sees Thee; therefore I retract, and repent in dust and ashes" (Job 42:5-6). Peter, in the presence of Christ, said, "Depart from me, for I am a sinful man, O Lord!" (Luke 5:8) Paul cried out, "Wretched man that I am! Who will set me free from the body of this death?" (Romans 7:24)

Did all of these men suffer from a destructive self-image? Hardly. The reason they were able to serve God with fervor is precisely because they understood that their significance, their self-worth, was derived from their relationship with God. They could "feel good" about themselves only because they had been forgiven and changed by the Lord of Glory.

The quest for significance is legitimate; we need a sense of well-being, but that comes only through our relationship with God. God confers this benefit upon us; we don't have to attain it in some other way. When Moses gave God a series of excuses why he should not have to return to

Egypt, God did not counsel him to improve his self-image. When Moses asked the question, "Who am I, that I should go to Pharaoh, and that I should bring the sons of Israel out of Egypt?" (Exodus 3:11), God did not give him a lecture on self-worth. Indeed, the Lord ignored the question entirely and simply assured Moses that He (the Lord) would be with him (v. 12). Then the Lord continued, "I AM WHO I AM" (v. 14). In other words, the question was not who Moses was, but rather who God is.

But don't we have innate worth? I like what Martin Luther said: "God does not love us because we are valuable; we are valuable because God loves us." And as for loving mankind unconditionally, instead the Scriptures teach, "The face of the Lord is against evildoers, to cut off the memory of them from the earth" (Psalm 34:16). Yes, as believers, we are permanently accepted before God through Christ, but even so, we can still displease the Lord, and when we do we fall under His discipline.

When psychology is blended with Christianity within the church, no one is told to stop believing in God. But when we imbibe such distorted notions, our concept of God begins to change. Those attributes of God that fit popular psychology are then stressed to the exclusion of other aspects of God's character. Soon we begin to believe in a God who just lets us be ourselves, a God who exists for our benefit.

A good example of this assimilation process is found in Robert Schuller's book *Self-Esteem—The New Reformation.* Enamored with the teachings of contemporary psychology, Schuller, who still wants to be known as an evangelical Christian, has replaced the Reformation doctrines of the depravity of man with a man-centered theology. He writes, "What we need is a theology of salvation that begins and ends with a recognition of every person's hunger for glory."[8] Whereas sin was traditionally thought to be against God, it is now defined as an act against man: "any act or thought that robs myself or another human being of his or her self-esteem."[9] And how shall we present the Gospel? "The gospel message is not only faulty but potentially dangerous if it has to put a person down before it attempts to lift him up."[10] In effect, we stand before God to be exalted, not to be abased.

Please take note: when Schuller accepts humanism's exalted view of man, he diminishes God. At that point, God exists primarily for man's benefit and not the other way around. The potter is molded into whatever image the clay desires.

We should not be surprised to find that Schuller has now taken the next step and accepted the techniques of Hinduism to find satisfaction and results through positive thinking. He argues that the meditation found in different Eastern religions is quite compatible with the Judeo-Christian religion. Both, he says, desire to overcome the distractions of the conscious mind. He regards these methods, regardless of their origin, as neutral from a religious point of view and hence beneficial to all. "The most effective mantras employ the 'M' sound. You can get the feel of it by repeating the words, "I am, I am" many times over. . . . Transcendental meditation is not a religion nor is it necessarily anti-Christian."[11]

We can confidently predict that in the days ahead secular psychology will make further inroads into evangelical Christianity. Subtly the idea will arise that we are able to perfect ourselves if only we better understand our latent resources. We will be hearing that our basic problem is not sin (indeed it is the teaching about sin that has given us a bad self-image); our problem is one of ignorance. We have not tapped our potential; we have not yet discovered our self-worth.

In C.S. Lewis' classic book *The Screwtape Letters*, the demon Screwtape instructs Wormwood about how to keep man confused. "Keep his mind off the plain antithesis between True and False. . . . What we want, if men become Christians at all, is to keep them in the state of mind I call

'Christianity And.' You know—Christianity and the Crisis, Christianity and the New Psychology, Christianity and the New Order. . . . Substitute for the faith itself some fashion with a Christian coloring.''[12]

Christianity and psychology is a marriage that tries to unite two competing faiths, two opposite worldviews. They can only be reconciled at the expense of Christianity. And as the New Age seeps in, the radical transforming power of Christianity is diluted. Someone said that we are accepting a gospel that "has an unobjectionable residue, with no power to save."

God is not a cosmic therapist who accepts me regardless. Nor am I my own God, able to access my own resources to find meaning in life.

The Bridge of Science of Mind

It's intriguing to think that whatever the mind can believe it can achieve. If my mind can control reality, as the New Age teaches, then I need not be locked into my present circumstances. Through a positive mental attitude and through faith—faith in my own essential godhood—whatever I want, I can have. In his book *The Magic of Believing*, Claude Bristol says, "By a full and powerful imagination, anything can be brought into concrete form."[13] Reality can be reordered by using images. Imagination can influence reality to such an extent that it becomes reality.

Meditation, we are told, is the key to power. Through it we can go into the depths of our inmost self to realize that "I am the power." Such ideas are based on the Eastern notion that the physical universe is an illusion and that reality can be reordered by the mind. Thought is the final reality, and since I am in control of my thoughts, I can basically produce whatever I want.

This New Age concept has infiltrated the church through the belief that we have the authority to receive anything we want from God. Through our faith, we can access God's power so that He is obligated to give us our wishes. Simply visualize what you want, and your imagination will force God to act. Through the power of the mind, based on the promises of Scripture, you can *manipulate God to bring it about.*

A television evangelist tells his audience each week, *"You can decree what God is obligated to do."* And how can we take that step of faith that obligates God to come through for us? It is done by making a $1,000 pledge to the ministry of this particular evangelist! This act will break any curse on your life and give you the authority to simply "name it and claim it!"

Hinduism says that I am God; therefore I have the right to manipulate reality through the power of the mind. Some Christians say that I have the right to manipulate the God and Father of our Lord Jesus Christ through the faith in my mind and a generous contribution. The difference between the two views is slight. Both affirm that I can control reality. I am ultimately in charge of what happens, all based on the visualization and faith within the mind. Either way, my will is done on earth and perhaps also in heaven.

This is the basis of the doctrine of prosperity that has gained acceptability in the last two decades. The argument goes like this: God wants all of His children to have both wealth and health in this life. We are children of the King and therefore have the right to be treated as such. The 2,000-year-old teaching of the church that we should be willing to deny ourselves and live in poverty for the sake of the kingdom is simply wrongheaded. Someone has aptly said that if Moses were alive today, it would not be said of him that he chose to "suffer affliction with the people of God" but that he chose to "suffer wealth, success, and popularity with the people of God."

And how does one achieve wealth and health? Through faith, yes, but also through visualization. "Form a mental picture of what you desire to achieve," writes Mack Douglas in his book *Success Can Be Yours.* "Place yourself in the picture. Experience the emotions of the moment. Bring to bear the use of the five senses. Feel, see, taste, smell, and hear it."[14]

Then he continues, "Say it is a new home. Draw all the details in your mind's eye . . . that's you standing by the Mercedes-Benz. Whose Cadillac, your wife's? . . .

"It's yours the minute you visualize it, and remember, the joy of the pursuit of earning it may be greater than living in it. . . .

"Think about it several times each day. Soon all your powers will be concentrated on its achievement."

We should not be surprised to discover that this technique works equally well whether one is a Buddhist or a Baptist. At root is the idea that we are able to achieve whatever circumstances we wish through creative visualization. Satan does his best to grant people their requests; he does not mind seeing us happy as long as we are deceived.

The New Age and Old Church have come together under the banner of faith and visualization. Christian celebrities can now justify their extravagant lifestyles and at the same time appeal for funds, assuring their listeners that giving to a particular organization is the best way to release faith. This act puts God in a bind so that He will have to honor their requests. Hinduism and Christianity have met under a distorted view of God's promises.

Yes, Christ did say that if we agree on earth concerning anything it would be given us. But this must be held in balance with a whole host of other Scripture passages that tell us things like, "If I regard wickedness in my heart, the Lord will not hear" (Psalm 66:18). James told his readers that they had not received from God because they asked selfishly: "You ask and do not receive, because you ask with wrong motives, so that you may spend it on your pleasures" (James 4:3). Paul was not delivered from his thorn, but rather was given grace to bear it (2 Corinthians 12:7-10). Suffering, Paul taught, is the mark of all who live godly lives.

Christ lived a life of poverty, having nowhere to lay His head. He also taught that the servant was not greater than his master. Here was a King's Kid who took the role of a servant and died in poverty and shame. If we are to follow Him, it is not through visualizing a Mercedes-Benz and expecting God to deliver it to us, nor even expecting God to help us earn the money for one.

If the gospel of health and prosperity were biblical, it is a message that could be preached in every country of the world. Try it in Russia, Rumania, and China, where believers are persecuted and discriminated against. Try it in Haiti and Ethiopia, and you would be laughed out of town.

The gospel of prosperity can flourish only in the United States and Canada where Christians enjoy freedom and capitalism has brought a measure of financial success. This gospel can only be preached by those who are themselves a product of Western commercialism.

Living the holy life is no guarantee that we can get whatever we want from God. Through visualization and even our own attempts at faith, we put God under no obligation to grant our requests. Only after we have sought His will and have bowed to His authority do we have a right to expect an answer, and even then it is subject to the Lord's sovereign will.

God is not a slot machine. We do not come to impress Him with our ability to visualize whatever we need and then expect to receive the jackpot. Prayer is above all a confession of humble reliance on the will and purposes of the Almighty.

The Bridge of Inner Healing

Satan was almost right when he said to God, "Yes, all that a man has he will give for his life" (Job 2:4). If the greatest fear of humanity is death, a close second is sickness which can easily rob life of its meaning. We are willing to try anything, no matter how bizarre, in an attempt to get well.

The notion that God wants everyone to be well has been

promoted by faith healers for many years. But with the advent of the New Age Movement, the doctrine of healing has taken on some new aspects. Once again, the biblical data is used to fit in with New Age theology and techniques.

There are a number of healing ministries based on the premise of Eastern religions, namely, that man has within himself the power of physical healing: psychoimmunity, acupuncture, hypnosis, and the like.

And if these techniques can be tapped to heal one physically, then we also have the resources to heal our emotional and spiritual needs too. Through visualization and recall, our memories and emotions can be healed.

Freud believed that man is controlled by impulses that lie buried in the subconscious. Hinduism and the New Age healers have accepted this idea, teaching that we must take a journey inward to achieve emotional wholeness. The secret is found in the proper use of the mind.

New Agers also contact spirit guides who lead them to awaken past pains and suffering. Through such help, patients are able to regress, even to the hurts sustained before birth. Thus, through uncovering experiences of rejection and even abuse, healing can be affected.

When these teachings are carried over into the church, they are of course given a biblical slant. Rather than using the guides of the New Agers, Christ is brought in to help with the recall and the emotional healing. Or, if the person is Roman Catholic, Mary performs that role.

Francis MacNutt, who teaches people how to be healed both physically and spiritually, describes his method this way: "If a person missed out on a mother's love in any way I ask Jesus (if the person is a Catholic) to send His mother Mary to do all those things . . . things that mothers do to give their children love and security."[15] We must be suspicious of techniques that work for all religions, techniques that draw on a force that belongs to no religion in particular.

Christ taught that the answer to a broken heart does not arise from within but from without, namely from the forgiveness, acceptance, and joy that comes through being rightly related to the Father. Christ Himself claimed to be a healer of broken hearts. On Calvary, He bore the emotional load of all those He died to redeem. "Surely our griefs He Himself bore, and our sorrows He carried; yet we ourselves esteemed Him stricken, smitten of God and afflicted" (Isaiah 53:4). By what authority can others make that claim? We can be thankful for counselors who help the hurting understand how Christ's provision can be applied. But there are no shortcuts, no techniques that can heal the scars of the past. If we have found a spiritual solution that works for all religions, we may be turning to the great imitator who desires to do all that Christ is able to do.

The Bridge of Spiritual Experience

New Agers think of the Bible as a repository of ancient wisdom, but they do not consider it the authoritative Word of God. If Satan is to make inroads into evangelical Christianity, however, his task must assume a new twist since we hold to the complete authority of the Bible in all matters of faith and practice. So the argument goes like this: yes, the Bible is the authoritative Word of God, but it is not sufficient for guidance in the day-to-day matters of life. We need individual and specific communication with God regarding personal decisions and problems. Therefore God communicates with us directly, bypassing His written Word. Soon visions, dreams, and extrasensory perception become a substitute for the Bible.

One television evangelist claims that he had a seven-hour conversation with Christ, during which they talked about the problems on earth and discussed decisions which he (the evangelist) was facing. Significantly, this man has also had some direct encounters with Satan who has tried to choke the preacher in his bed. Unfortunately, this man does not see the connection between the two events. Without question the Jesus that appeared to him was a manifestation of a demonic spirit who took the name "Jesus Christ."

Dozens of such stories abound all over the world. Some claim that they have met Christ; others say Mary has appeared, bemoaning the spiritual state of the church on earth. Some claim communication with the saints of the past. Apparitions, messages, and revelations are all claimed in the name of Christ.

We must remember a basic principle: whenever we seek direct communication with Christ, we are in danger of meeting spirits who claim to be Christ—antichrists, if you please. Demons have been known to *appear in whatever form they are expected to.*

Christians are often deceived at this point because the communication they receive may be beneficial and even scriptural. One woman who took guidance from a voice she heard thought it was from God because it would tell her to go to church or to do good to her neighbor. She did not realize that evil spirits frequently make scriptural statements to deceive. The evil spirit said to Christ, "You are the Son of God!" (Mark 3:11) Even though the statement was theologically sound, Christ rebuked the spirit for speaking. We are not to communicate with spirits, even if they should happen to speak the truth.

Think of Satan quoting verses back to Christ—countering the Son of God directly from His own Bible!

Everything that is miraculous is not necessarily from God. Keep in mind that Satan's great desire is to duplicate whatever Christ can do. The evil one will answer as many prayers as he can; he will perform miracles, relay helpful messages, and often appear under the name of someone else. We should not be ignorant of his schemes.

The Bridge of Ecumenism

As already explained in a previous chapter, the New Age Movement knows that it is impossible to unite the religions of the world on the basis of a theological creed. No attempt is made to hammer out an agreement on the doctrine of God and salvation. But New Age leaders insist that this is not necessary. The conviction is that *although a universal theology is not possible, a universal experience is possible—indeed, the religions of the world must unite on experience alone.*

Please note: the New Agers teach that we can all have the same experience regardless of what we believe. No need to worry about sticky points in theology; all of us can take a different route to spiritual reality. Remember, there are as many ways to reach the divine as there are spiritual exercises in the world. Even experiencing God through Christ is valid, just as long as we don't say that Christ is the *only* way to the Ultimate One, that is, God.

All of this is consistent with the basic premise that man does not need a redeemer but is capable of redeeming himself. Through enlightenment and the journey within, he is able to perfect himself. The creeds of Christendom are actually barriers to the vast expanse of spiritual experience that lies before the one who is willing to cast aside the intellectual content of Christianity and embark on the fascinating journey of spiritual consciousness.

Evangelicalism has not yet drifted that far from its theological underpinnings. But constantly we're hearing statements like, "Let's just get away from theology and enjoy the Lord." Or, "Let's not study a creed but experience Christ."

Such anti-intellectualism and disdain for rigorous theological precision can only hasten the eventual acceptance of New Age teaching within the evangelical community. Yes, theologians can be boring; some people have over-intellectualized their faith. And, yes, it is possible to know God without having a good grasp on theology. Yet for all that, it is theological debate and hard study that has kept the church from being blown away by every wind of doctrine. It is safe to say that we cannot recover the spiritual dimension of the church unless we also recover the intellectual dimension—the doctrines that have guided and guarded the church throughout its turbulent history.

We are bombarded with the notion that the great need of Christendom is for unity, regardless of our theological differences. If our doctrinal disagreements were minor, such pleas would be more understandable. But they are not. The differences between Roman Catholicism and Evangelical Protestantism, for example, are vast.

Contrary to what the New Agers say, the church cannot be united on the basis of experience but on the basis of theology, the essential doctrines that undergird the Christian worldview.

Where Is the True God?

One day in the year 850 B.C., Ahaziah, one of the kings of Israel, fell through the upstairs floor of the palace into a lower room. According to the biblical account in 2 Kings 1, he injured himself and became ill, and longed for a speedy recovery. He sent messengers to inquire of Baal-zebub, the god of Ekron. These servants were to ask this foreign god whether the king would recover from his illness.

The Prophet Elijah met the messengers and asked them this question: "Is it because there is no God in Israel that you are going to inquire of Baal-zebub, the god of Ekron?" (v. 3) The prophet then said that the king would surely die.

Ahaziah obviously did not like that prediction. So the king sent 50 messengers to Elijah to persuade him to change his mind. The prophet did not change his mind, but called down fire from heaven to destroy the messengers. The king was still unconvinced and sent another delegation of 50 who suffered the same fate. When the third delegation came, Elijah went to visit the king, but the verdict did not change. Ahaziah the king would have to die.

Elijah again asked: "Is it because there is no God in Israel that you have sent to Baal-zebub?"

The question for us is similar. Is it because we are dissatisfied with God's dealings in our lives—is it because we want spiritual experiences and quick results—is this why we are willing to tolerate a foreign conception of God within our ranks? Why do we want a God who is a cosmic therapist? A slot machine in the sky? A servant who cures all our ills? A friend who sends us special communication whenever we think we need it?

These and a dozen other conceptions of God are gaining popularity within the ranks of historic Christianity. At root we are rebelling against the sovereign God of the Bible. We want a God who will do our bidding, a God of instant results. Subtly we are being introduced to the god of this world.

Our challenge as believers is to prove to the world that the God whom we serve is eminently satisfying. C.S. Lewis says that in the Psalms, God is presented as the "All-satisfying Object."

Through our lives and witness we have the privilege of saying to a confused world, "O taste and see that the Lord is good; how blessed is the man who takes refuge in Him!" (Psalm 34:8)

Those who taste of the true God do not imbibe the sweet potions of false gods. Let us never trust the god of this world, even when he brings us gifts.

Chapter Nine

Infiltrating the Home

*A*n uproarious ghost comedy. There hasn't been any-thing remotely like it since *Ghostbusters*. An irresist-ible treat. . . . In this house if you have seen one ghost, you haven't seen them all." Rated PG.

This ad, which arrived in our home today via the daily newspaper, is aimed at the children of America—children who, for the most part, question whether ghosts actually exist but are willing to feel the excitement of encountering them if they did. No doubt the movie will be seen by hundreds of thousands if not millions of America's youth. They will accept the comedy in stride and, according to the ad, "hear voices of laughter from the hereafter."

Just good clean fun and excitement? Possibly, but then possibly not. The message of the movie is clear: there just may be a spiritual dimension to the world; there may be disembodied spirits who exist and who are scary but fortunately quite harmless. In fact, some of them may even be there to help us, like Casper the "friendly ghost."

Then there is the movie *Willow* released by George Lucas, the mastermind of the *Star Wars* trilogy. Costing $35 million, this movie makes the religious statement that God is both good and evil, and in the end, says one reviewer, good prevails over evil by 12 to 11. Yes, in the end good triumphs, but not by much. Pantheism, not theism, is the message that millions of children receive when they see this science-fiction extravaganza.

A recent movie tells the story of a hero who arrives in heaven and falls in love with a beautiful young woman who must return to earth reincarnated. The young man must now decide whether he will go back down to earth with her or stay in heaven. He risks all and leaves heaven to be with her.

But isn't a lively imagination God's gift to a child? Yes it is, but like other gifts it can be misused to accept the lies of the devil. Our imagination is perhaps the most powerful aspect of the mind. The ability to visualize what has not yet happened or to invent and plan what we want to happen is a part of our creativity. Indeed, our imagination is so powerful it can easily captivate all of our energy and attention. We speak of a leader as "having a dream," that is, he is consumed by something that has not yet happened. Such is the power of the imagination.

A basic axiom is that *we are both attached and motivated by what we imagine.* That attachment can lead to an obsession. The imagination can eventually take over; it becomes an extension of ourselves. The child's imagination becomes the bridge into the kingdom of Satan. The fantasy becomes the reality. A child who enjoys seeing occult movies or playing occult games *will eventually take on the desires of the characters he is watching.* And why not? He is watching what he *desires* to see.

That's why seeing movies about ghosts, dabbling in occult paraphernalia, and playing games based on occult associations can become a doorway into satanic control. Satan wants to recruit children to come under his banner.

The entertainment industry is his best method of indoctrination.

By creating characters who have supernatural powers, children are drawn into a distorted occult fantasy world. For example, the cartoon character He-Man is the Master of the Universe; he has more power than Christ according to some of the children who watch the series. He can control a castle with ghosts and squash rebellion by mere force. He is, in effect, omnipotent and virtually omnipresent. He performs one supernatural feat after another. And for him, might makes right.

According to Phil Phillips, a mother and her son were riding in the car listening to a sermon on the radio. The minister started to pray, "Our Lord God, Master of the universe." The little boy in the backseat corrected him, "Mommy, God isn't the master of the universe; *He-Man* is."[1] Another boy comforted his mother who was in a near auto accident by assuring her, "Don't worry, Mommy. He-Man would have saved us." Phillips also tells the story of a girl who ran around the house doing everything in the power of Grayskull, a demon-possessed castle in the He-Man series.

As Christians, our imagination must come under the control of the Holy Spirit. Since God judges our thought life, we are told, "Watch over your heart with all diligence, for from it flow the springs of life" (Proverbs 4:23).

God's scrutiny of the imagination is confirmed in the verse, "Then the Lord saw that the wickedness of man was great on the earth, and that every intent of the thoughts of his heart was only evil continually" (Genesis 6:5).

Interestingly, at the building of the Tower of Babel (where the New Age got its start), the Lord said, "Now nothing will be restrained from them which they have *imagined* to do" (Genesis 11:6, KJV, italics added). Even back then the theory was, "Whatever the mind can believe, the mind can achieve!"

The point is that we should not use our imagination to

visualize anything that is contrary to God's standard of decency and purity. Men use their imaginations today to create a host of images that are contrary to God's will. And soon they are controlled by these evil images.

New Age Games

The *Chicago Tribune* carried a story of a 17-year-old California boy who washed up on a San Francisco beach, a suicide victim. Then there was the 12-year-old who shot his 16-year-old brother; two teenagers in a suburb of Chicago committed suicide by running the family car in a closed garage. In Texas, a drama student shot his teacher, and in Kansas a 14-year-old shot the school principal and wounded three students.[2]

What do these tragedies have in common? In each case the youths had been avid players of "Dungeons and Dragons," a game that requires no boards or moving pieces, just an active imagination and a sharp mind. In many cases the youths had left behind gruesome drawings and peculiar notes seemingly inspired by the game. The children's parents contend, and thousands of others agree, that this game can lure impressionable young people into violence, the occult, insanity, and death. One father, whose son shot himself through the heart after a "death curse" had been placed on him during the game, said, "You do not casually play this game, just like you do not casually take heroin."

During the game the players take on the identities of medieval warriors who collect treasure and build strength and power as they battle their way through monster-filled mazes. The monsters can inflict punishments ranging from infecting flesh to poisoning to whipping and immolation. Characters can cast "insanity curses" on one another that include sadomasochism, homicidal mania, and suicidal mania.

Dr. Thomas Radecki, a University of Illinois medical psychiatrist, says that the game causes a lot of young people to turn to violence against others and themselves. He continues, "It causes a desensitization to violence . . . in a lot of cases, the kids start to live in this fantasy world. Unfortunately a lot of these kids are not finding their way out of these dungeons."[3] A private detective in Dallas says he has investigated a half-dozen suicides linked to the game. In each case, he said, the youths had collected "Dungeons and Dragons" literature, drawn gruesome fantasy cartoons, dabbled in occult rituals, and withdrawn from their families and friends before killing themselves.

A student who stopped playing the game because it drew him into the occult said that the game rewards you if you steal and if you kill. Then he added, "This fantasy can be much more appealing than reality. . . you become dissatisfied with reality and become wrapped up in the fantasy. . . . The player-character attachment is so close and personal . . . that if your character dies, there is an extreme emotional trauma."[4]

Already in 1985, it was estimated that four million Americans were playing the game "Dungeons and Dragons"; today that figure is much higher. And of course there are other such games on the market. One is called "Skeltor," where the chief character holds an occult symbol in his hand, and the comic book that comes with the game in effect teaches that Satan, not God, is the creator of the world.

Walk through a toy store and you will see occult symbols everywhere. *The Saga of the Crystar Warrior* action figures combine violence and the occult. The back of the toy box reads, "Somewhere in the universe exists Crystalium, a world where magic reigns! After a cosmic demon war, twin brothers, Crystar and Moltar, became rulers of Crystalium." These brothers have to choose between order and chaos and in the process are transformed into superhuman creatures by the mystical power of wizards. The crystal, as seen here, is used in the occult practice of necromancy, the practice of talking with the dead.

If psychologists are right in saying that when one lives in

the realm of fantasy for a period of time the lines dividing reality and fantasy become blurred, we have reason to be concerned about the toys and cartoons American children are absorbed with. Dr. Joyce Brothers says that war toys remind children that adults often settle disputes with force and violence.[5] Thus studies indicate that children who play with such toys exhibit a greater degree of aggressive behavior such as kicking, biting, punching, and general rule-breaking.

Remember the words of the student absorbed in "Dungeons and Dragons": "The fantasy can be much more appealing than reality." That, as we have learned, is precisely the basic premise of the New Age Movement—reality exists in the mind, not in the material universe. Consequently our God-given gift of imagination can be misused and become a bridge between ourselves and the occult world.

Thousands of Christians are having their children stolen from them by Satan, right in the comfort of their own homes. Though we would fight to the death if an intruder came into our home to physically abduct them, we often allow them to be captured in other equally destructive ways. The devil's "evangelistic" strategy has filtered into our living rooms via TV and "fun and games."

Infiltrating the Schools

"Twenty-five first-graders lie in motionless silence on the classroom floor," writes Frances Adeney. "The teacher intones soothing phrases to aid relaxation. Within moments, the meditative journey begins. The children imagine the sun . . . they are told to bring the sun down from the sky and into their own body . . . until their bodies are ablaze with light."[6]

Then follows instruction on how to become perfect, by filling the mind with knowledge until their whole body becomes a beam of light. Eventually they contain all of the light in the universe. Now they are at peace and are perfect. They are told that they are intelligent, magnificent, and *contain all the wisdom of the universe within themselves.*

This is the guided imagery that is taking place in a Los Angeles public school classroom. The teacher is Dr. Beverly Galyean who has developed three federally funded programs of confluent education in the Los Angeles public schools. She describes confluent education as a "holistic approach using thinking, sensing, feeling, and intuition."[7]

Here are the premises:

1. We are not individuals but part of the universal consciousness. At base this consciousness is love.

2. Each child contains all the wisdom and love in the universe. This is known as the "higher self." The children are taught to say, "I am a perfect person and a student." They can tap into a universal mind through meditation and contacting *spirit guides.*

3. Each student creates his or her own reality by choosing what to perceive and how to perceive it. The physical world is an illusion; the reality of evil is denied.

First-graders also are introduced to spirit guides, though Dr. Galyean remarks that "we call them imaginary guides." During the year, when a child needs comfort or advice, he is instructed, "Ask your guide."

Galyean sums up her philosophy:

> Once we begin to see that we are all God, that we all have the attributes of God, then I think the whole purpose of human life is to reown the Godlikeness within us; the perfect love, the perfect wisdom, the perfect understanding, the perfect intelligence, and when we do that, we create back to that old, the essential oneness which is consciousness. So my whole view is very much based on that idea.[8]

How can such full-blown occultism be taught in our schools—especially when religion is not to be brought into the classroom? Frances Adeney, herself an educator, says that she attended conferences led by Dr. Galyean. Hundreds of public school teachers participated, responding enthusiastically to these ideas.

Then there is the educational philosophy of Jose Silva that is used by some teachers, often with great success. One of his goals is to have his course in mind control taught to all the children in this country. He believes it is possible to tap higher sources of knowledge because of our latent "spiritual energy." Strictly speaking, no one talks with the dead but, in his words, "We're contacting the programming, the impressions, recordings made by these people when alive."[9] So rather than just learning about Abraham Lincoln, one can tap into his knowledge directly by a guided tour into this mystical field of energy.

Space forbids more examples of how Eastern occultism is infiltrating our schools. The bottom line is this: whereas in past eras there were few people who specialized in being mediums, *these forms of occult power are now being taught to whole classrooms of children.* The destructive sorcery of Edgar Cayce is now being practiced by first-graders who are taught to consult their "guides." Parents should be aware that to take children to school might mean that they are placed in the hands of the enemy.

Needless to say, Christians parents have to stand against the intrusion of Eastern religion into the classrooms of America. If not, we become an ally with Satan in his plan to rule the world.

The Infiltration of Music

New Age radio stations are becoming popular around the country. An article in a May 1985 edition of *Newsweek* says that this soothing music is based on a "mystical world-view and a striving toward a relaxing musical mood."[10] The titles of the songs tell the story: "Cosmic Energy" and "Easy Is Right," to name a few. The reason for the tranquil sound is to build a bridge between the conscious and the subconscious and to "excite our spirituality."

This kind of music may not be harmful to Christians who do not use it to enter into a mystical mood of spiritual experience. But with the increase in record sales and the proliferation of New Age radio stations, we can expect such music to further perpetuate the Eastern worldview among those looking for an entry point into some form of spirituality.

The demonic nature of hard rock music is less subtle. There is a direct connection between secular hard rock and demonic practices such as witchcraft and sorcery. The lyrics peddle the New Age doctrines of magic, transcendental meditation, and the pantheism of the East. Much of this music is written under the influence of drugs.

Interestingly, our English word *pharmacy* is derived from the Greek word *pharmikia* which means "sorcery." In the Book of Revelation the Greek word is used in passages such as 9:21, which reads, "And they did not repent of their murders nor of their sorceries nor of their immorality nor of their thefts." The use of drugs and sorcery are related for an obvious reason: drug users escape into the world of fantasy and imagination where evil spirits are only too eager to invade the mind. Indeed, drug users often appeal to occult powers.

Michael Haynes in his book *The God of Rock* sees five major themes that keep repeating themselves in hard rock music: (1) sex, (2) drugs, (3) rebellion, (4) false religion, and (5) Satan.[11] For lack of space, only the last two will be considered here.

Many of the rock groups openly promote the religion of the New Age, not only by their lyrics but by using symbols of Satan and demon worship. As Haynes points out, "It seems that if groups do not have a 'god' of some sort to project, they simply find one. There are so many idols presented in the symbolism on album covers that a fairly exhaustive study of FALSE RELIGIONS in America could be constructed from these alone."[12]

Rock music is intended to break down any resistance

that one may have toward immorality and indecency. The minds of millions are thereby conditioned to accept the philosophy of the music. As Mick Jagger of the Rolling Stones put it, "We've had their bodies . . . now we want their minds."

Many of the lyrics are so obscene that they cannot be legally played over the radio or television, though the law is often flaunted. Many of our teenagers have their bedrooms equipped with a stereo so that rock records can be played loudly and repeatedly. There they learn about demon possession, drugs, and immorality.

What do the lyrics say? Here is a song by Ozzy Osbourne entitled "Diary of a Madman." Notice the references to demon possession:

A sickened mind and spirit
The mirror tells me lies
Could I mistake myself for someone
Who lives behind my eyes?
Will he escape my soul,
Or will he live in me?
Is he tryin' to get out or tryin' to enter me?[13]

Or consider these words which set forth Satan as God. The song is entitled "The Number of the Beast" and is found on an album of the same title.

Woe to you, of earth and sea . . .
For the devil sends the beast with wrath;
'Cause he knows the time is short.
Let him who has understanding
Reckon the number of the beast;
For it is a human number,
It's the number six hundred and sixty-six
Satan's work is done!
666 the number of the beasts!
Sacrifice is going on tonight![14]

In addition to the blatant teaching that Satan is God, some lyrics also promote the New Age notion that we are God. Listen to a statement by John Denver: "Apollo taught me to fly. Oh, how he taught me to live! Some day I'll be so complete I won't even be human. I'll be a god."[15] Apollo is the major deity of the sun, moon, and stars.

Through music, many children today are being stolen; that is, their spiritual values are being taken away and replaced with the god of rock. David Crosby put it clearly: "I figured the only thing to do was to swipe their kids. By saying that, I'm not talking about kidnapping; I'm just talking about changing their value systems, which removes them from their parents' world very effectively."[16]

Yes, the mind has awesome powers, created by God for the purpose of knowing Him and serving Him in this world. With it we form ideas, make decisions, and communicate our beliefs and preferences. One aspect of the mind is the imagination that enables us to leave reality and think creatively about that which *is not yet*. Our imagination enables us to plan and to take future contingencies into account. So far, so good.

But unfortunately, because we are fallen creatures, the imagination of man is often the hotbed for hatching evil schemes. Via the imagination we can imagine doing evil that we tell ourselves we would never do in real life. The man who might not commit the physical act of adultery can do it repeatedly in his imagination without anyone knowing it; the person who is angry can commit murder without fear of being arrested. And the person who is overcome by greed can visualize himself surrounded by uninterrupted ease without any concern for the poor around him. For good or for ill, our imagination is perhaps the most powerful aspect of the human mind.

A Biblical Response

The imagination has tremendous power for evil. But fortunately, the imagination can also be used constructively. We can focus the mind on biblical realities. Moses, you will recall, was able to leave the luxury of the palace and identify himself with the sorrows of his own people because he "endured as seeing Him who is unseen" (Hebrews 11:27).

Abraham was willing to leave the security of his homeland and go to a strange country because "he was looking for the city which has foundations, whose architect and builder is God" (Hebrews 11:10).

Paul specifically instructs us to "keep seeking the things above, where Christ is, seated at the right hand of God" (Colossians 3:1).

The use of the Christian's imagination is one of the most powerful motivations for holy living. To have our minds renewed by the Holy Spirit and the Word is, in fact, the secret to authentic Christian living.

How does the Christian's power of imagination (visualization, if you will) differ from the use made of these powers in the New Age Movement?

Christian "visualization" has several characteristics. First, we should not visualize any image of God or Christ. This is to break the second commandment, for the image in the mind can be just as idolatrous as the image of stone. And as noted earlier, this can lead to direct communication with evil spirits. Instead we must meditate on the *promises and character of God.*

Second, we should never try to empty the mind so as to think about nothing in particular. The Christian should always meditate on specific *content* and never try to think of nothing (as in transcendental meditation). Those who meditate *in the law of the Lord* are blessed.

Third, we should use our imaginations to create that which has not yet come to pass—such as an artist or builder might do. We do this not because the imagination has the power to fulfill the reality, but in order to set about doing God's will in an orderly way. An illustration is close at hand. When we set out to write this book, we as authors sketched the broad outlines of what we wanted to include and exclude. We visualized what we wanted the final product to look like. This helped us accomplish our goal. Imagining the goal motivated us to achieve it.

Some people have a much more creative imagination than others. They see a need and think of a plan to solve it. Some Christian leaders are great simply because they see more than others through the eyes of faith. That is using the imagination for the glory of God.

Finally, we can enjoy those feats of the imagination (entertainment, for example) that induce us to think thoughts that are consistent with holy living. There is some latitude as to what may be proper or improper for each individual, but the basic rule is nonnegotiable: we should watch only those programs, play only those games, and listen only to music that is pleasing to our Heavenly Father.

The lines between the followers of God and the followers of Satan will eventually become clearly drawn. As the spirit of Antichrist gains in power, more and more people who call themselves Christians will not be able to make up their minds about who they belong to.

Satan has infiltrated the home, fully intending to carry away as many children as he can. Christ contrasted Himself with this enemy when He said, "The thief comes only to steal, and kill, and destroy; I came that they might have life, and might have it abundantly" (John 10:10).

Chapter Ten

Infiltrating Politics

On April 25, 1982, newspapers in 20 major cities worldwide carried a full-page ad which in part read:

THE WORLD HAS HAD ENOUGH...
OF HUNGER, INJUSTICE, WAR.
IN ANSWER TO OUR CALL FOR HELP
AS WORLD TEACHER FOR ALL HUMANITY
THE CHRIST IS NOW HERE

The advertisement went on to say that Christ would be recognized by "His extraordinary spiritual potency, the universality of His viewpoint, and His love for all humanity. He comes not to judge but to inspire."

This world teacher, the ad announced, is Lord Maitreya, known to Christians as the Christ, to Jews as Messiah, to Buddhists as the Fifth Buddha, to Muslims as the Iman Mahdi, and to Hindus as Krishna. The ad stated that these are all names for the same person.

This teacher would bring peace to the world through brotherhood and sharing. Through his enlightenment, earth's problems would be solved.

Though many people didn't take this ad seriously, there is a network of organizations committed to bringing about a unified world order to address our major problems with creative solutions. Leading the pack will be a world ruler with the charisma to unify all religions and to weld a political structure with the muscle to forge global subjection. He will be both priest and king, both messiah and world emperor.

Remember that this ruler will derive his strength from the same source as Adolf Hitler, who controlled Germany with such hypnotic magnetism that his leadership was practically irresistible. Several books have been written that document Hitler's involvement with Eastern occultism. Indeed, the swastika is a Hindu symbol of divinity. Hitler's mentor, Dietrich Eckart, predicted that Hitler would be a world leader. Hitler was manipulated by invisible forces which he called "Unknown Superiors," in reality, demons who both controlled and terrorized him. Hitler told his friend Rauschning that he was founding the Man-God order and that splendid being would be an object of worship. Rauschning said of Hitler:

> One cannot help thinking of him as a medium . . . the medium is possessed . . . beyond any doubt, Hitler was possessed by forces outside himself . . . of which the individual named Hitler was only the temporary vehicle.[1]

Hitler's hatred of the Jews and his belief in the superiority of the Aryan nations were undoubtedly derived from Hinduism with its belief in the caste system—the idea that certain people are born inferior to others and that weeding out the undesirables is part of good leadership.

This New Messiah will be the Antichrist of Revelation 13.

He will be worshipped on earth and will have awesome authority.

New Religion

The New Messiah will usher in a religion that will counterfeit Chrisitanity point by point. Instead of prayers, there will be mantras; instead of preachers, there will be gurus; in the place of prophets, there will be psychics; the Ten Commandments will be replaced by a new set of commandments for the present age; instead of the Holy Trinity, there will be an unholy trinity. This ultimate blasphemy is detailed in Revelation 13, where the dragon corresponds to God the Father; the first beast takes the place of God the Son; and a second beast, who causes the inhabitants of the earth to worship the first beast, corresponds to the Holy Spirit.

Here at last, Satan has achieved his most cherished desire; namely, to rule the world. He will receive recognition and worship; he has finally installed himself as king and savior.

Alice Bailey, in her book *The Externalization of the Hierarchy*, speaks candidly about the need to reorganize the religions of the world to offset their "out of date theologies, their narrow-minded emphasis and their ridiculous belief that they know what is in the Mind of God . . . in order that the churches may eventually be the recipients of spiritual inspiration."[2]

New Government

Now that Satan's puppet is in place, he will be able to control the world through a vast financial network based on stringent controls. No one will be able to buy or sell without the "mark of the beast." Those who challenge his authority will be put to death.

Predictions about such a world system have been made for years in New Age literature. H.G. Wells said that there would be a worldwide revolution consisting of a great multitude and variety of overlapping groups "all organized for collective political and social and educational as well as propagandist action." Wells continues:

> It will be a great world movement as widespread and evident as socialism or communism. It will largely take the place of these movements. It will be more, it will be a world religion. The large loose assimilatory mass of groups and societies will be definitely and obviously attempting to swallow up the entire population of the world and become the new human community.[3]

Marilyn Ferguson in *The Aquarian Conspiracy* writes that a "leaderless but powerful network is working to bring about radical change in the United States. Its members have broken with certain key elements of Western thought, and they may even have broken continuity with history."[4]

Benjamin Creme in his book *The Reappearance of Christ and Masters of Wisdom*[5] makes the astounding statement that Christ has been back on earth since July 1977 and that a single, global religion will be started and probably flower within the next 20 years. When asked whether the advent of a single world religion will annoy the hierarchies of all the current orthodox religions, he admitted that they would be the last to accept this new order, but "it will come anyway, because it must. We will begin to live as 'potential gods.'"

In New Age literature there is talk of a necessary cleansing process that will be needed to quell the opposition of those who resist the new religious/political order. Those who refuse to be initiated into Satan's kingdom by taking the mark of the beast will be eliminated.

What will be the goals of this new religiopolitical alignment?

1. *Nationalism must end.* The public schools must foster beliefs in global citizenship and the interdependence of

nations. Moves must be made to eliminate the pledge of allegiance from the classrooms of the nation.

2. *A new credit card system* that will eliminate the cumbersome monetary transactions of today. The world now has the capability to do this with computers. We can expect there will be attempts to standardize the currency so that the world will actually become one global village, able to do business with more ease and equity.

The January 1988 edition of *The Economist* carried a story entitled, "Get Ready for a World Currency."[6] The article said that governments and businessmen are becoming weary of exchange rates. "Thirty years from now, Americans, Japanese, Europeans, and people in many other rich countries and some relatively poor countries will probably be paying for their shopping in the same currency," the article begins. All that we need, the author says, is a few more economic setbacks and exchange rate upsets. The boundaries between different countries will disappear and the world money supply will be controlled by a central bank. The advantages for trade and efficient government are obvious. Of the new currency, which the writer identifies as "the phoenix," he says, "This means a big loss of economic sovereignty, but the trends that make the phoenix so appealing are taking that sovereignty away in any case."

Like it or not, we are moving toward a world currency which is the means by which Satan's inspired leader will eventually rule the world.

3. *A world food supply* authority that would redistribute the food of the world to "even out" the inequities that now exist.

4. *Emphasis on disarmament and the "elimination of nuclear weapons."*

All of this is to be done under the banner of love and peace. "Universal brotherhood" will be the slogan that will capture the aspirations and hopes of millions who will be drawn into the centrifugal force of this movement with the best of intentions. The goals of this movement will be stated in such a way that it will appear that *only the most obstinate and belligerent could possibly oppose such noble ideals.*

This, then, is the culmination to which all the various strands of the New Age Movement are headed. The tributaries do eventually flow into a single river. Here is the apex of the godhood of man. At last the problems of the world will be overcome—and with a *spiritual solution.*

Under the guise of laudable slogans, the deification of man will reach its most striking affirmation. The predictions of both the Old and New Testaments regarding a coming world ruler will be fulfilled.

Needless to say, to pull this off, this ruler will have to have at his disposal the unquestioned control of the peoples of the world. That is no small task, given Arnold Toynbee's assessment, "Blessed is the nation that has no history, for history is the record of war." How can man's nature, which has been so violent and selfish, be transformed to bring about a unified, just society? Besides, at least three powerful religions believe in theism, that there is a God independent of the universe. Christians, Jews, and Muslims will find it difficult to accept the belief that each person is God. Alice Bailey speaks of the need for the gradual dissolution of the orthodox Jewish faith with its "obsolete teaching." Indeed, all religious fanatics will have to be defeated, according to Bailey, who writes:

> This inherent fanaticism (found ever in reactionary groups) will fight against the appearance of the coming world religion and the spread of esotericism. For this struggle certain well-organized churches through their conservative elements (their most powerful elements) are already girding themselves. . . . The coming struggle will emerge within the churches themselves; it will also be precipitated by the enlightened elements who exist in fair numbers already, and are rap-

idly growing in strength through the impact of human necessity.[7]

How then can the New Order be brought about? The answer comes in two parts. First, we must remind ourselves that the New Agers believe in the evolution of man. He is getting better and better, and the last step of the evolutionary process is his spiritual transformation through the New Consciousness, the journey inward, the trip to Eastern religions where rationality does not exist. Many who belong to organized religions will "see the light." We can expect that the resistance will not be as great as one might imagine. Brigham Young of the Mormons, for example, already asserted back in 1873, "The devil told the truth (about godhood). I do not blame Mother Eve. I would not have had her miss eating the forbidden fruit for anything."[8] Mormonism has always asserted the deity of man. It could easily assimilate the new enlightenment.

Second, there is education. Moves are afoot to teach globalism in the public schools. Not only is this being done by including New Age ideas in the curriculum (transcendental meditation, for instance) but by teaching the need for the unification of the countries of the world. A state legislator, appearing on an Omaha talk show, said:

> We have to control church schools because fundamental, Bible-believing Christians do not have the right to indoctrinate their children in their faith, because we, the state, are preparing all children for the Year 2000, when America will be part of the One World Global Society and their children won't fit in.[9]

New Agers are not naive enough to believe that everyone will accept the dawn of this new day. Some will oppose the emerging New Order. For these, there is another solution: intimidation, starvation, and liquidation.

This is not our theory, but the expressly stated agenda of

the New Agers who candidly admit that drastic measures will have to be implemented to keep people in line. Alice Bailey in her book *The Externalization of the Hierarchy* stresses the need for disarmament as the New World Order continues to emerge. This, she says, will not be optional. Does this mean, however, the total elimination of nuclear weapons? Not at all, or at least not until the New World Order is firmly in place. She says nuclear weapons should be used by an organization such as the United Nations to:

> enforce the outer forms of peace, and thus give time for teaching on peace and on the growth of goodwill to take effect. . . . The atomic bomb . . . belongs to the United Nations for use (or let us rather hope, simply for threatened use when aggressive action on the part of any nation rears its ugly head). It does not essentially matter whether that aggression is the gesture of any particular nation or group of nations or whether it is generated by the political groups of any powerful religious organization such as the Church of Rome, who are as yet unable to leave politics alone and attend to the business for which all religions are responsible—leading human beings closer to the God of love.[10]

Make no mistake: if and when the New Order comes, it will not be because everyone will voluntary fall in line. Those religions that will not accept the lie that man is God will be systematically eliminated by whatever means is necessary. In the New Age, disarmament will be the guise used to get the nations of the world to surrender their sovereignty to an authoritative global political machine, which will in turn use those weapons (if necessary) to force everyone, especially the religious objectors, to get on board with the new agenda.

Understand Satan's methodology: there is a vast difference between his advertising and the product that the purchaser receives. George Orwell called it *newsspeak*. Talk about disarmament but plan to use weapons on those who refuse to accept your agenda. Campaign for individual freedom but plan to eliminate the freedom of those who don't toe the line. Affirm the value of humanity while at the same time you favor the systematic killing of the unborn and the eventual death of millions.

The Invisible Government

Much has been written about the machinery that is already in place to bring about the emerging world order. It is no secret that the Trilateral Commission and the Council on Foreign Relations is actively working to introduce changes that would bring about globalism, that is, the unification of the nations of the world. For years Barry Goldwater has kept a file on these organizations and in his book *With No Apologies* discusses the hidden agenda of these powerful groups. Of the Trilateral Commission he writes, "It is intended to be the vehicle for the multinational consolidation of the commercial and banking interest by seizing control of the political government of the United States."[11] He concludes by identifying the areas of power that the commission seeks to control as political, monetary, intellectual, and ecclesiastical.

The Bible too predicts the ultimate globalization that the New Age will bring about.

When Will This Happen?

Christ taught that we know neither the day nor the hour of His return. Yet we are also told that we should be able to discern the "signs of the times." Each generation has those who believe that their age is the last, yet here we are approaching the year 2000 and Christ has not yet appeared.

Theories about the end of the age are many. Some writers firmly predict that we are indeed living in the last age. Though this may be so, we must caution about being too certain. Some of the older readers of this book will recall that a spate of books appeared before the end of World War II affirming that Hitler was the Antichrist and the end of the world was near. Surely such false predictions should be sufficient to heed the warning that in matters of prophecy, it is better to say too little than too much! Good advice for all Christian writers.

Though the conditions of the world today appear to fit the pattern predicted in the Bible, we must be realistic enough to realize that the same conditions may appear in a later era. Antichrist may be alive today; or perhaps he is yet to be born in the future.

With these disclaimers in mind, I must point out, however, that there are two events that will be necessary in order for the World Ruler to control the entire globe. The first is a general drift toward disarmament, which will give impetus to the notion that world peace is attainable. In a word, the Western nations will be lulled into a false belief in the peace process. Second, there will have to be a worldwide monetary collapse in order to force nations to relinquish their autonomy.

In 1987, the United States and the Soviet Union signed a peace treaty that calls for the dismantling of some nuclear weapons in Europe. The famous historian Arnold Toynbee made the statement, "No nation has ever made weapons it did not use." This treaty is an exception to Toynbee's observation. For the first time in history nations are actually destroying weapons rather than using them! This agreement is widely heralded as a major breakthrough in East-West relations and a step forward to world peace. Many believe that it is but the beginning of a series of treaties that will bring about the end of nuclear armaments.

Interestingly, the Bible predicts that the Day of the Lord will begin when the nations of the world will be basking in the sunshine of a false peace. The Day of the Lord, Paul says, will be like a thief in the night: "While they are saying, 'Peace and safety!' then destruction will come upon them suddenly like birth pangs upon a woman with child; and they shall not escape" (1 Thessalonians 5:3).

Whenever the world cries "peace" we can be quite sure it is a false alarm. When the world is in a state of euphoria, congratulating itself for having attained peace, the treaty will fall apart. Whether this is the period of peace spoken of by Paul or whether there will be another one to come, we do not know. Of this we are certain: a false peace will precede the Day of the Lord.

In October 1987, Wall Street suffered "Black Monday," when the Dow Jones Industrial Average fell more than 500 points on a single day. Despite dire predictions, this event has not had a significant effect on the economy of the Western nations. Something far worse will have to happen before the world is brought to its economic knees.

Back in 1982, a weekly investment magazine called *International Moneyline* predicted such a colossal economic failure.

> Reaganomics will fail . . . it's just about over. The casino is still open, but the hour is late . . . we're on the brink of disaster.
>
> After the financial panic, the economy will fall faster and farther than anyone now expects . . . the world is headed for an economic abyss and there is literally nothing that anyone can do to stop it. . . .
>
> There has never been a more certain scenario.[12]

Yes, the world is headed for an economic collapse. But here again, we must be cautious about a time frame. The economy of the United States still could remain strong for many years. Eventually, however, the gloomy predictions will come to pass.

What does this have to do with the rise of Antichrist? There is simply no way that the nations on earth will surrender their sovereignty unless the entire world is in an "economic abyss." The Antichrist will become a hero and literally worshipped because he will pick up the pieces of a collapsed world economy. He will walk into a vacuum created by the destruction of the world markets. The nations will welcome his brilliant leadership and gladly accept the stringent controls that he will enforce at the pain of death. He will make extravagant promises and will, to a large degree, make good his claim.

Antichrist will make these promises based on the New Age philosophy that all men are God and therefore quite able to solve their own problems. Out of the ashes of economic defeat, hope will rise once more. The economic reform will be widely accepted as proof of Antichrist's claims.

The second beast of Revelation 13 (who corresponds to the Holy Spirit) causes all to be given a mark on their right hand or on their forehead "and he provides that no one should be able to buy or to sell, except the one who has the mark, either the name of the beast or the number of his name" (Revelation 13:17). Thus economic control is assured.

By now the Antichrist will have presented himself as God in the temple. Signs and wonders will be a daily occurrence. Those who follow will experience the beginnings of prosperity. But it will be for only three and a half years (Revelation 13:5). Then the Antichrist will break a treaty he had made with the nation of Israel, not realizing that this breach of promise is the beginning of the end.

Eventually God comes on the scene to unleash His wrath upon a rebellious world. The nations are in an uproar, angrily fighting against the God of Abraham, Isaac, and Jacob. But He is angry too, for mankind has insulted him by worshipping themselves and in reality crowning Satan as the god of this world. The anger of man and the anger of God collide in what is the worst destruction in all of history. The Book of Revelation teaches that there will be three sets of judgments—seals, vials, and trumpets—that will bring about incredible suffering and pain. God will heap fire, hail, and wind upon the earth. The waters will turn to blood and the sun will scorch all vegetation. Demons, the entities described by New Agers, will roam the earth to persecute all of mankind.

Will this lead men to repentance? Incredibly, the answer is *no*. "And the rest of mankind, who were not killed by these plagues, did not repent of the works of their hands, so as not to worship demons, and the idols of gold and of silver and of brass and of stone and of wood, which can neither see nor hear nor walk; and they did not repent of their murders nor of their sorceries nor of their immorality nor of their thefts" (Revelation 9:20-21).

Please note that they will not repent of their sorcery—those who trust in crystals still will trust in them; those who consult their channelers to get in touch with their ascended masters still will trust in them. Others will continue to consult their horoscopes and ouija boards. A few still will try to create their own reality by the power of positive thinking and transcendental meditation. They'll hang tenaciously to the notion that "whatever the mind can believe, the mind can achieve." They still will prefer to believe in their own godhood than to repent in the presence of the living God.

The Glorious Return of Christ

Finally, the nations of the earth will gather together for the final battle called Armageddon. At all costs, Satan must exterminate Israel; God's chosen people must be destroyed so that the purposes of God are defeated. But alas, these plans are not to be. The true World Ruler, Christ, comes to claim His kingdom.

> But immediately after the tribulation of those days the sun will be darkened, and the moon will not give its light, and the stars will fall from the sky, and the powers of the heavens will be shaken, and then the sign of the Son of Man will appear in the sky, and then all the tribes of the earth will mourn, and they will see

the Son of Man coming on the clouds of the sky with power and great glory. And He will send forth His angels with a great trumpet and they will gather together His elect from the four winds, from one end of the sky to the other (Matthew 24:29-31).

Benjamin Creme believes that when the New Messiah (actually Antichrist) comes, he will prove to be taller than Jesus of Nazareth; the Christ of the New Testament, Creme believes, will lose the final contest.

Not so. The Christ born in Bethlehem 2,000 years ago will come to destroy the New Age Messiah; all of His enemies will be crushed. He comes to deal out retribution to those who do not know God. "And these will pay the penalty of eternal destruction, away from the presence of the Lord and from the glory of His power" (2 Thessalonians 1:9).

The beast and the false prophet will be thrown into the lake of fire, and then those who worshipped the beast will be cast into the same place of punishment where they are tormented day and night forever and ever (Revelation 19:20-21).

Thus the Age of Aquarius will come to a close.

Chapter Eleven

New Age—New Opportunities

We should be thankful that the New Age Movement is not creeping up on us unawares. Books, magazines, and tapes exposing the deceptions of Satan can be found in every Christian bookstore. But there is a hidden danger in all this attention the enemy is receiving. *Christians can fall into the danger of overestimating Satan's power.*

The sin of unbelief can be committed in two ways: we can either minimize the power of God, or we can thoughtlessly magnify the power of the devil. Either way we give unnecessary ground to the enemy. Whenever we feel overwhelmed, we must remember that Satan is not God's competitor. They are not even in the same league.

The challenge is to see the many opportunities that have come to the church with the dawning of this New Age. There is evidence that God may be opening the hearts of many in the Western world to the good news of the true Gospel. This is not the time to run and hide, waiting for the end of the world. This is the time to walk through new doors, to seize new opportunities and defeat Satan at his own game.

Gardeners recognize that there are four vital conditions that must be balanced for the growth of healthy plants. The soil must be open or receptive to the seed; there also must be light, moisture, and nourishment. When these factors come together in proper proportions, hearty plants are practically assured. But of course, if there is too much sunshine, the plants will wither; too much moisture and they will drown; too much plant food and they will burn up. And if the soil is hard, the seed will lie exposed and not germinate.

Church growth experts tell us that cultures and societies go through phases of either hostility or openness to the Gospel of Jesus Christ. A "people group" previously closed to the Christian message may suddenly become receptive and thousands be converted.

Reasons for the change in spiritual climate are difficult to pinpoint, though several recurring factors have been identified. The one that is most reliable is defined by George Hunter. He writes, "Populations in which any religion is growing should be perceived as open and searching for something. . . . Whenever we see a growing non-Christian religion, we can be sure that the people in that place are potential receptors of the Gospel."[1]

To be specific: along with the growth of religions like Islam, cults such as the Unification Church, or the diversified appeal of the New Age Movement, there is the potential of a parallel spurt in growth of evangelical Christianity. People are searching, looking for answers to ultimate questions, and taking steps to meet their felt needs.

The rationalism of 19th-century Europe came to America amid great promises of scientific and cultural advancement. Along with it came the seeds of what we call secular humanism, the belief in atheistic evolution, and the notion that there was but one substance in the universe—namely, matter. There was no room for God, souls, angels, or demons.

As spirituality was separated from society, atheism flourished. Those who still claimed to believe in God lived as though He did not exist. All this led to one of the most materialistic societies known to man. The American dream of owning your own home with a two-car garage and plenty of money left over for clothes, food, and entertainment is now a reality for most of us. Increasingly, people have turned to pleasure to satisfy the spiritual vacuum. Immorality and drugs are prevalent among all strata of society. And now following hard on the heels of these pseudogods comes the New Age Movement, promising contact with a *religious* god who nonetheless doesn't judge anyone. The exhilaration of using the power of your own mind to achieve whatever you want is too much to resist.

Materialism cannot satisfy for one good reason: man was created to have fellowship with God. Though a fallen culture taught him to disbelieve in the supernatural, man's own nature would not let him be at peace with such a worldview. And since neither drugs nor immorality could quench his thirst for the divine, he became a ready prey for a movement which promised to put him in touch with himself—a movement that declared man himself was God. Contact with this spiritual dimension could be had simply by tapping the latent powers of the mind.

The unprecedented interest in spiritual phenomena should be a megaphone that awakens a slumbering church to the realization that people are now open to talk about the supernatural. Gone are the days when a belief in miracles was regarded as the remains of a superstitious age. If it is true, as the opinion polls suggest, that 42 percent of the American people claim to have talked with the dead, we are living in an age of incredible openness to spiritual reality.

The evangelical church could, if fully committed to Christ, make gigantic inroads into territory that is deceptively claimed by Satan. Most people who dabble with New Age techniques are not hardened satanists bent on rearranging the present social structure. They are just ordinary citizens who are turned off to organized religions and are trying to find something that gives them spiritual fulfillment. On the surface, at least, they are as open to Jesus Christ as they are to Shirley MacLaine.

What must we do if we want to capitalize on the spiritual harvest that is so ripe in Western civilization? Figuratively speaking, Satan often shoots himself in the foot. His schemes frequently backfire. He inspired men to crucify Christ only to discover that Christ's death was a decisive victory over him; he tried to snuff out the church in China only to learn that persecution caused its unprecedented growth (the estimate is 40 million believers in China today). He has a grand design to introduce Hinduism into Western society, *but we have the potential of using this open door to confront millions with the truth.*

There is no doubt that we can take some giant strides for Christ if we recover three biblical characteristics of genuine Christianity.

The Enjoyment of God

A woman who attended one of Dr. Lutzer's seminars on the New Age Movement was anxious to talk. "I've been involved with everything you have talked about," she began. "I have been a master in Zen meditation—so good at it that I taught it in seminaries throughout Europe.

"Eight years ago I became a Christian and since that time I have never doubted the reality of Christ. But I have a question: why have I not found the same, sharp ecstatic joy in Christianity as I had in Zen? My biggest temptation is to return to meditation to recover that feeling of euphoria. Why don't I have the same kind of a spiritual high with Christ?"

A fair question. That Christianity is the only true religion is believed by millions of us who are evangelical Christians.

Why can't we promise converts a greater high than Zen or even drugs? Why or why not?

The Westminster Confession of Faith declares that the chief purpose of man is to "know God and enjoy Him forever." John Piper in his excellent book *Desiring God— The Meditations of a Christian Hedonist* says that the framers of the confession did not intend us to understand that knowing God and enjoying Him were two separate responsibilities of man. Rather, we could read that the chief end of man "is to know God *by* enjoying him forever."[2] The saints of the past, says Piper, were unashamedly hedonistic—they believed that God was to be enjoyed. Consider this hymn by Bernard of Clairvaux:

> Jesus, Thou Joy of loving hearts,
> Thou Fount of life, Thou Light of men,
> From the best bliss that earth imparts
> We turn unfilled to Thee again.

Unless we as Christians are able to capture the experiential aspect of our theology, we will never be able to convince contemporary man that we have found that which satisfies the deepest hunger of the human heart. Christ invited the thirsty to come to Him to drink. If He is incapable of keeping His promises, or if we have not found how to tap into His resources, then we will be forced to defend our faith only on an intellectual level. But our generation craves more, and we should be able to witness from a heart that knows something of the "fullness of joy."

In 1978 a Gallup Poll conducted by the Princeton Research Center revealed that 60 percent of the unchurched people agreed with this statement: "Most churches and synagogues have lost the real spiritual part of religion." A corollary statement won equally high approval: "Most churches and synagogues today are too concerned with organizational as opposed to theological or spiritual issues." For the majority of people, Christianity is not a belief that enables people to enjoy God, but rather a heavy, tedious hierarchy interested in perserving the past and supporting itself.

C.S. Lewis was indeed right when he said that the Psalms presented God as the "All-satisfying Object." The Psalmist David would have agreed. He wrote, "Thy lovingkindness, O Lord, extends to the heavens, Thy faithfulness reaches to the skies.... They drink their fill of the abundance of Thy house; and Thou dost give them to drink in the river of Thy delights" (Psalm 36:5, 8). And again, "Delight yourself in the Lord; and He will give you the desires of your heart" (Psalm 37:4).

We can go to the person who is into transcendental meditation and the person who is experiencing the intoxication of drugs, and say, "Let me show you how you can really enjoy God." Indeed, if a person knows nothing of the enjoyment of God, could not this be evidence that he or she is not a believer at all?

Why then did that woman at the seminar say that the subjective experiences of Zen seemed to be greater than the joy of God? There are several differences between the spiritual experiences of the New Age and that of Christian joy.

First, the world operates on the premise, "If it feels good, it must be right." But, of course, that premise is wrong—it's the fourth spiritual flaw mentioned earlier in this book. We cannot decide what religion is right by the high it gives its participants.

Drugs can give one a euphoric experience; a man who commits immorality with another man's wife may talk about the elation of their sexual liaison. A man who murdered a young girl said, "It felt so good." And the list can go on. *The intensity of the experience is no guarantee of its long-term value, nor does it prove that it is based on truth.*

We believe that an experience is ultimately only as good as its source. If Christ is the truth, as He claimed, then we must put our trust in Him regardless of whether our experience of Him is euphoric or low-key. One man finds what he believes to be a diamond in the dust, but later discovers the stone is a fraud. Another finds what looks like a stone and it turns out to be a genuine diamond. It matters little as to which of the men had the most elation at the time of his find.

Both Christ and demons are able to give humans a spiritual experience. Christ bears witness to the truth; demons speak only lies (except when they can use truth to enhance their deceptions). Does it really matter which of the two give their servants the greatest spiritual high? The source of the experience is the ultimate test of its validity. That's why Christianity is based on faith in an authoritative Word from God, not feelings.

Second, Christian joy always results in a concern for others; it is never a private experience that exists solely for self-pleasure. A young woman who was led to Christ through a neighborhood Bible study made the startling comment, "I've done a lot of crying in the last six months since becoming a Christian." Pressed for an explanation, she continued, "Before I was a Christian I was happy because I was selfish. In those days it didn't matter who was in the hospital or who was getting a divorce; I just went on in my merry, self-centered way. Now I have 'new eyes' so I visit people in the hospitals, and I cry over people's marital problems."

Does Christianity make people more miserable than it finds them because they now have a concern about those around them? The young woman answered that question by adding, "But even with all the crying, I have never had such a sense of peace; it's not like the fun I used to have—this is better and deeper."

What is the difference between the experience of the Eastern religions and the experience of the true God? One is self-centered, the other is people-centered; one seeks the experience itself, the other seeks the true God, and the emotional experience connected with it is secondary. Christian joy comes when we look away from ourselves— first to God, then to others.

Finally, and most importantly, the experience of the true God never has negative side effects. Those who come out of some form of the New Age Movement often say that although their first few experiences seemed to be satisfying, they soon learned that there was a dark side to the "transformation of consciousness." There was always a price tag. Eventually the payments became more than the client could bear.

Samuel Zwemer was famous for his missionary work among the Muslims. He and his wife and children worked in the Persian Gulf for many years with little response. The daily temperature often reached over 100 degrees in the shade. In July 1904, both of his daughters, ages four and seven, died within eight days of each other. Fifty years later he looked back on this period and wrote, "The sheer joy of it all comes back. Gladly would I do it all again."[3]

That is the strength of true joy. Faithful to the calling of God and lost in service to others, this is the testimony of a fulfilled life. Here is a key contrast between the gladness of the world and that of a worshipper of God: "Thou hast put gladness in my heart, more than when their grain and new wine abound" (Psalm 4:7).

The Enjoyment of Others

Cultists know that the best lure to recruit new converts is to meet one of mankind's most basic needs: love and acceptance. Engraved on the heart of every child is the desire to be nurtured and loved by two parents. But as all of us know, the homes of America are breaking apart. Young people want to have friends; they crave a loving heart and a listening ear.

Is this need new in the history of mankind? No, but it is greater today than at any other period of time in this nation's history.

New Age—New Opportunities

Let me explain: in previous generations, people had their social needs met by their families which, for the most part, stayed together for better or for worse. If a child felt emotionally deprived, he probably had grandparents who lived in approximately the same geographical area. Beyond that, there was the neighborhood, where everyone knew everyone else. There was a sense of interdependency, a feeling of community. If church consisted of nothing more than attending a service or two on Sunday, that was sufficient. All of one's emotional needs were met in the ways just described.

We live in a new day. Two factors have deprived our nation of the love and security that is so necessary for sociological and emotional stability. First, there is divorce. It is estimated that one-half of all the children born this year will at some time live with a single parent. The rejection and anger that is felt by the children of this generation is beyond description. This emotional wound runs deep and takes special sensitivity to heal.

Second, there is mobility, which has uprooted practically every family. Children are reared thousands of miles from their grandparents, aunts and uncles, and cousins. People do not know who their neighbors are. They can live next to one another in a high-rise building for years without bothering to become acquainted. We are characterized by hyperindividualization; the social fabric of the family and community has been torn apart.

We are driven into our narrow worlds by the competitiveness of business and the privatization of pleasurable pursuits, such as watching television or renting the latest video. We insulate ourselves from others by riding to work alone and entering our garage with an automatic door opener that gives us anonymity right to the front door of the house or apartment.

This has resulted in a tremendous emotional vacuum in the lives of millions of unfulfilled Westerners. Churches that take steps to fill this void will be successful in halting the drift away from organized religion to the lure of the New Age sects. If we are to speak to this generation, it must be within a community of love. Jesus said, "By this all men will know that you are My disciples, if you have love for one another" (John 13:35).

Why are so many New Age seminars well attended? Part of the reason is that people are looking for spiritual fulfillment, but the other half of the story is that they are lonely and are looking for meaningful personal relationships.

Satan, who knows the needs of humanity better than we do, has latched onto the fact that his gospel is best promoted through the means of small groups, seminars, and retreats. There in face-to-face confrontation, people are open to new ideas; they are willing to listen, interact, and believe.

There are three social needs which we can call the three "C"s of community. To be fulfilled, people must feel *comfortable* among their peers. They need acceptance and secure friendships.

Second, there is *commitment*, a sense of loyalty and stability. This is the "social cement" that gives us the ability to cope with the problems of life.

Finally, there is *contribution*, the sense of satisfaction that comes when feeling needed. The need for personal significance can only be met when people know they are contributing to the legitimate needs of others.

Through such small groups we can say to an aching world, "Come see the power of God on display among His people." Amid their defeats, failures, and joys, a stability comes from knowing that Christians belong to God and to one another. There is an excellent remedy for personal failure. God forgives the sins of those who repent and believe the Gospel.

Some churches may be busy distributing Bibles, but they do not demonstrate how the Bible works. The Gospel does not merely tell us how we can get on good terms with God, but how we can get along with one another. It is God's guidebook on community relationships. We should be able to say to our friends, "Come to church with me and see how this Book applies to all of us."

Such an atmosphere, placed in our open and searching society, will accelerate the growth of the church.

The Enjoyment of the Word

How can love for God and others become a part of our daily experience? Communication is the key within marriage; it is also the key in our relationship with God. He has written us a love letter that must be read and assimilated. A person who has no love for the Word of God has no love for God. To refuse communication with the Almighty strains the relationship just as much as frozen lines of communication stifle a marriage.

Christians believe in meditation. In fact, it is not possible to be a growing Christian without this daily habit. The man who is blessed is described: "But his delight is in the law of the Lord, and in His law he meditates day and night (Psalm 1:2). The difference between this and transcendental meditation is quite obvious. Biblical meditation means that we think about specific content—the written message of God. Transcendental meditation, as we have seen, aims at thinking about nothing at all. The one informs the mind; the other seeks to destroy it.

Experts tell us that people retain 10 percent of what they are told, as in a sermon or a classroom. But people will retain 90 percent of what they discover for themselves and share with someone else. There is a way in which we can capitalize on this clue to better learning. The next few paragraphs will describe and illustrate a method of Bible study that can change your life. You will be excited with what you learn, and you will remember much more than you do by simply reading the text. Contrary to popular opinion, it is not true that "a chapter a day keeps the devil away!"

Whether you are in a small-group Bible study or on your

own, *you can find meaningful spiritual food from the Bible each day.* Spend 15 or 20 minutes in the text daily and you will notice a gradual change in your spiritual walk.

Here is our challenge. For one month, do this exercise each day: read a few paragraphs of the Bible and begin by answering three *observation* questions.

1. *What verse or truth did you like best?* Your opinion matters. Furthermore, the truth you select may be an interesting reflection of some need you have that particular day.

2. *What did you like the least?* We know that the entire Bible is the Word of God and all of its truths are relevant. But there may be some parts of it that do not strike us as being particularly helpful or that may even be confusing.

3. *What did you not understand?* It is not necessary to understand everything in a passage to profit from it. Perhaps reading the text in another translation will help, or possibly a commentary would shed some light. Sometimes we have to be willing to wait for more light on a particular text.

Now answer three *reflective* questions:

1. What did you learn about God?

2. What does this passage tell us as believers to do?

3. Choose a favorite thought that you can take with you today.

Before you say this approach is too simple, try it! Better yet, invite a friend who is interested in the New Age to study the Word with you. Those who have an interest in spirituality should be willing to study a Book that touches on virtually all aspects of the spirit world. And it does so with understanding and authority.

Dozens of Bible study helps are available at your local Christian bookstore. The World Home Bible League has a course built around the six questions listed earlier. It's entitled, "Happiness Is . . . " and seeks to reinforce each step of the Bible study process with concrete examples and selected exercises.

If the believing church got back to three basics—the

enjoyment of God, the enjoyment of one another, and the enjoyment of the Word—the assault of the New Age Movement could be curtailed, if not halted altogether.

Yes, prophecy *will* be fulfilled; the Antichrist *will* arise and deceive the nations. But this is not an excuse for an anemic fatalism that lets Satan take over without a fight. The true Gospel can and will destroy the false gospel when the two are brought into sharp, deliberate conflict.

For the church to back off at this critical hour is not a credit to the ascended Christ. This is the hour to enter into Satan's house, bind him, and set the captives free.

The battle is not ours but the Lord's. Let's make sure our feet are firmly planted on His side of the boundary line.

Chapter Twelve

The Destructive
Power of the Gospel

housands of people who have been ensnared by the teachings of the New Age Movement are waking up to the realization that they are now hostages to Satan and his demons. Others are still deceived, believing that they have come to a new understanding of themselves by tapping into the hidden powers of the universe.

Let's think about the subtlety of Satan's trap and then point the way out of his mystical maze. Fortunately, Christ's power can destroy his clever grip on the lives of those who admit their need for help.

The Power of Deception

To keep people in bondage, Satan's strategy is that of duplication; he counterfeits virtually everything that God does. If you seek a religious experience, he will give it to you; if you need guidance, you will receive it; and if you want healing, that is available too. Because all of these benefits can be received without repentance and humility, *he offers a shortcut to spiritual reality.*

This explains why those who hear voices often find the messages helpful and soothing. Satan will come as close as he can to giving advice that sounds as though it comes from the true God. The blurring of the distinctions between right and wrong, between the individual and God, and between rationality and irrationality—all of these confusions serve his purpose.

A young woman who rebelled against the Christian faith and was involved in a long list of New Age practices eventually became physically incapacitated. Yes, she was a Christian, and yes, she now sought deliverance. But she was hearing a voice, which she interpreted to be the Holy Spirit, giving her words of comfort: "You must endure all these things because of your disobedience. But I will be with you through it all." Because of this, she did not immediately seek deliverance, concluding that her emotional and physical problems were inevitable.

Only later did it become clear to her that this was not the voice of Christ but of an evil spirit impersonating the comforting ministry of the Holy Spirit. Fortunately, this confusion was eventually identified.

Notice how subtle the deception has become. It is true that God often uses Satan to discipline wayward believers. Consider these examples: King Saul had an evil spirit from the Lord trouble him because of his jealousy toward David (1 Samuel 18:10); the immoral believer in Corinth was turned over to Satan for the "destruction of the flesh" (1 Corinthians 5:5); Paul himself was given a satanic thorn in the flesh (2 Corinthians 12:7). The fact is that God often uses Satan to discipline those who go astray. How then can we tell the difference between an experience that is brought upon us illegitimately by Satan and an affliction that must be simply endured for the cause of Christ?

In this case, there were two reasons to believe that the voice this woman heard was demonic. First, the messages mingled comfort with *condemnation*. The voice frequently quoted verses of Scripture, but they were always words that increased the guilt she already felt. *Satan continued to condemn her for sins in her past that she had already confessed and forsaken.* Whereas the Holy Spirit confirms the forgiveness of God, Satan always continues to question it. *Guilt* is one of his most persistent weapons.

Second, we can recognize the work of Satan when a person is spiritually bound, without joy and inner peace. In the case of Saul and the immoral person at Corinth, God used the evil spirit to intensify their rebellion and guilt that they might be brought to repentance. But once such a person comes to the place of honest repentance and renunciation, Satan's work ceases. Then the believer can command Satan to flee.

Paul's experience was in a different category. His thorn in the flesh was physical, not spiritual; it was to keep him humble. But he was not a victim of depression and spiritual uncertainty. That's why he said he could now "boast in [his] weakness" (2 Corinthians 12:9).

The point is this: once sin has been confessed and forsaken, there should be a sense of cleansing and joy, a release from satanic oppression. "If we confess our sins, he is faithful and just to forgive us our sins and to cleanse us from all unrighteousness" (1 John 1:9). This young woman not only continued to experience guilt despite her confession, but also lived with an emotional cloud of uncertainty and confusion.

Fortunately, God did not allow this young woman to be misled indefinitely. Through prayer and Christian counsel she realized that this bondage to Satan was unnecessary. Then one day while listening to a pastor's message about the power of Christ, two wicked spirits unexpectedly manifested themselves and then left her body. She was free after years of bondage to occult powers.

Like a wolf who waits for a sheep to stray from the flock, Satan keeps his eye on those who have had bitter experiences with Christianity. He builds a barrier between the individual and his parents; between the individual and the church; and most importantly, between the individual and God. Children refuse to discuss their experiences with their parents, thinking that they belong to the old order and would not understand. They cut off Christian friendships and do not attend church. All of their waking moments are spent preoccupied with their new way of perceiving reality.

Soon the victim actually believes that he is a part of an elite group, those who have special knowledge, those who have "seen the light." He actually develops a feeling of superiority, the notion that he has insight others lack. If his friends ask for a logical explanation, he can ignore their requests and protest that they simply do not understand. The enlightened do not need explanations.

Think of how thick the walls of this prison have become: these individuals believe they are having a genuine spiritual experience with whatever god there is; they are proud of the inner wisdom others lack. These barriers are used to *effectively cut them off from the very people who could help them back to freedom.*

Let's review Satan's strategy.

First, there is *duplication*, the attempt to counterfeit the work of God at every level.

Second, there is *isolation*, the severing of all friendships that could help the individual back to rationality and the Christian faith.

Third, there is *guilt.* At first the individual may feel obligated to pursue the "enlightenment" now that he has begun, a feeling that he owes it to himself to move deeper toward the transformation of consciousness. If he should become aware that he is now trapped by satanic powers, the focus of the guilt now shifts. *He feels obligated to pay Satan his dues.*

Fourth, there is *fear,* the feeling that even if this path is wrong, the way back is so painful it is not worth the cost.

I've met people who have told me that they feared having demonic powers leave them. They would be bereft of their "friends," shorn of their emotional or spiritual crutch-es. They were terrified of a direct confrontation with Satan. Even as believers, they continued to accept these lies.

If you ask whether born-again Christians can have de-monic afflictions because of involvement with New Age phenomena, the answer is yes. Those converted out of the occult may not be entirely free after their conversions. And those who dabble with Satan's techniques after becoming Christians can also be ensnared by the devil.

But fortunately, many people become weary of paying their dues to this enemy. They hear that Christ has come to set the captives free; His mission to earth was to destroy the work of the devil. They realize that at the Cross, Christ won the decisive victory over Satan. "When He [God the Father] had disarmed the rulers and authorities, He made a public display of them, having triumphed over them through Him [Christ the Son]" (Colossians 2:15).

For those who have come to this realization, Satan changes the nature of his tactics just a bit. When his vic-tims realize that Christ is stronger than he is, he replies: "Yes, Jesus is stronger, but complete deliverance is not worth the hassle. If you continue to be my servant, I will give you certain favors. Let's make a deal."

When a person is finally willing to renounce all compro-mises; when he or she is willing to face the truth, no matter what the implications may be, spiritual freedom becomes a possibility.

Yes, there is a way out.

The Power of Christ

How does an individual come out of the grips of satanic bondage? For some it happens quickly; for others it takes time. But for all who desire it, victory is sure. Apart from the first step, the others listed here are not necessarily in the right order for everyone. Some people have to go through this procedure many times; others may alternate between freedom and bondage.

1. The personal acceptance of Christ as Saviour.
Many people who were brought up in Christianity have ended up in some form of the occult simply because they did not experience reality in "organized religion." Indeed, we should not be surprised, because no one experiences reality in organized religion!

Usually, these people lack a personal relationship with Jesus Christ. Perhaps they had all the facts—they knew the Bible stories and even a bit of doctrine—but they had never transferred their trust to Christ alone for their salvation. They knew virtually nothing about the immediate work of the Holy Spirit in the human heart.

Sometimes children who are brought up in Christian homes say a prayer for salvation at an early age. As they grow older, their parents tell them that they were saved because they prayed to "accept Jesus" years before. But the child enjoys no intimacy with God. There is nothing but the empty form, the bare beliefs without any reality.

Others were brought up in churches that stressed that grace is communicated through the sacraments. They believe that a ritual can convey salvation to those who are baptized or participate in the Lord's Supper or the Mass. Needless to say, they are left spiritually destitute, unable to find the reality their hearts crave. They are candidates for New Age propaganda.

When someone doubts his or her salvation, the wisest course of action is to *now* make sure that the complete transfer of trust has been made to Christ alone for acceptance and forgiveness. Through proper counsel and the witness of the Holy Spirit, the doubts can be taken away.

2. There must be a complete renunciation of all involvement in occult practices along with submission to Christ as Lord.
Jesus is Lord over all wicked spirits, but He must be crowned Lord in the individual's life as well. Such honest submission takes Satan's territory away from him. He may insist that he has a right to continued obedience to his

practices, but the believer need not cling to such a lie.

Let me illustrate Satan's strategy from the animal kingdom. I'm told that out in the wild, several bull moose may have a bitter battle to see who takes charge over the herd of females. However, once the victor has been established, the defeated animals never challenge his authority again.

Satan, once he has won several key battles, wants his prey to think there is no use trying to become free. The victim is overwhelmed by the strength of the enemy and may feel too afraid or too weak to challenge his captor's authority. So the person may simply end up doing the bidding of Satan and his demons.

This cycle of intimidation must be broken. And it can be, by pointing to Christ's decisive victory over the devil. Indeed, even before the Cross, Christ saw Satan fall from heaven like lightning (Luke 10:18). *Now he is free to control only those who believe his damning lies.*

If you have been into the New Age, list those practices that you have been involved in and renounce them one by one. Put your entire life under the sovereignty of Christ.

3. You must receive the strength of the body of Christ.

Satan wants us to think that we have to fight our battles alone. We've already learned that he keeps his allies separated from those who would be able to help them out of spiritual bondage. That isolation must be broken.

Most sins of the flesh cannot be overcome without the help of other believers. A person caught in the grip of pornography seldom comes to freedom alone. Many will testify that sharing their bondage with a few other trustworthy believers was the path to freedom and victory. God does not allow us the luxury of living the Christian life successfully on our own. Confessing our sins to one another has two benefits: (1) we benefit from other people's prayers, and (2) our humility makes Satan flee.

4. All routes back to the occult must be closed.

Those who have been involved in the occult must be

careful not to become ensnared again. This can happen more easily than it appears. The possibility of fascination with palm reading, astrology, and transcendental meditation can be easily revived, especially when one is going through a bitter disappointment or a severe trial. The temptation is to say, "God has not helped me. Maybe I should help myself."

Jesus told a story about a demon who departed from a man and sought rest but found none. So the evil spirit said to itself, "I will return to my house from which I came" (Luke 11:24). Christ continued, "Then it goes and takes along seven other spirits more evil than itself, and they go in and live there; and the last state of that man becomes worse than the first" (v. 26).

The empty life must be filled. We are exhorted not only to put off the old man, but also to put on the new (Colossians 3:8-10). The principle of replacement runs throughout Scripture. This means we must be reading and meditating on God's Word every day.

Daily Safeguards

How can we protect ourselves from Satan's attacks? The answer is to put on the whole armor of God so we can withstand the lure of the enemy.

The six pieces of armor mentioned by Paul in Ephesians 6:13-17 are well known by most Christians. What is less known is how to put the pieces on to insulate ourselves from the schemes of the devil.

Let me list these pieces, showing their practical application to spiritual freedom.

1. We are to gird our loins with truth (v. 14).

Deceit of any kind gives opportunity for Satan to gain a foothold in our lives. This may involve lying, which is usually done to cover other sins. A person who has learned to manipulate others to make himself look good will soon become the pawn of the devil.

Those who are involved with immorality and who continue to cover their sin when it is pointed out to them will repeat the same sins. The reason is because their untruthfulness allows Satan repeated entry into their lives. Truthfulness is necessary for victory.

2. We are to put on the breastplate of righteousness (v. 14).

All believers have the righteousness of Christ credited to them legally. The fact that we are exhorted to put on this breastplate means that Paul has in mind the application of this righteousness to our lives.

This is done by affirming that Christ is our righteousness and standing on that fact when Satan uses guilt to manipulate us.

Jesus, Thy blood and righteousness
My beauty art, my heavenly dress

3. We are to have our feet shod with the "preparation of the Gospel of peace" (v. 15).

The Gospel, which is the power of God for salvation, destroys Satan's power. Believers who are ready and willing to share the Good News make inroads into Satan's kingdom and thereby learn how to defeat the enemy.

4. The shield of faith will extinguish the "flaming missiles of the evil one" (v. 16).

When the ancient Romans fought, they used arrows that had been dipped into pitch. The tips were lit and shot at the enemy with the intention of beginning a fire behind enemy lines. To counter this weapon, shields were often dipped in water to extinguish the flames.

Satan's strategy is to inflame our passions—whether it be lust, gluttony, alcoholism, pride, or whatever. These burning passions can only be overcome by faith.

Specifically, how do we put on this shield? First, we must not fall into the trap of overestimating Satan's power and therefore thinking that our bondage to these lusts is inevitable. Second, we must focus on Christ who has defeated Satan and sin. The shield of faith means that we daily affirm Christ's victory and take advantage of our place with Him, "far above all rule and authority and power and dominion and every name that is named, not only in this age, but also in the one to come" (Ephesians 1:21).

5. We are to put on the helmet of salvation (v. 17).

The protection of the mind is essential in spiritual warfare. We must know the full extent of our salvation and use the Gospel message to keep ourselves from accepting messages from the kingdom of Satan. In the early church, Ananias and Sapphira decided to tell a lie to make themselves look good in the presence of the Jerusalem congregation. Peter asked them, "Why has Satan filled your heart to lie to the Holy Spirit?" (Acts 5:3)

We can put on the helmet of salvation by our commitment to the truthfulness of the message of salvation with all its implications. This is best done through memorizing Scripture and singing hymns of praise to the Lord.

6. We must take up the sword of the Spirit, which is the Word of God (v. 17).

We all know that Christ used the Word of God when He was tempted by the devil. Satan did not leave when the first verse was quoted nor the second. Luke tells us Satan eventually departed "until an opportune time" (Luke 4:13).

Many Christians who know how to use the Bible against the devil become discouraged if there is not an immediate spiritual victory. They think that the Word of God does not work as they had hoped.

Remember that we can only exercise the authority of the Word when we ourselves are under its authority. When the seven sons of Sceva thought they could exorcise demons in the name of Jesus just as Paul had done, the demon replied, "I recognize Jesus, and I know about Paul, but who are you?" (Acts 19:15) Then the man in whom the evil spirit lived leaped on them and subdued two of the men so that they fled out of the house naked and wounded (v. 16). Here is an example of what can happen when one uses the Word of God or the name of Christ without being in subjection to its power.

Satan must eventually flee when we stubbornly persist in standing on the Word after putting ourselves under its authority. But the battle may be intense and the attacks repeated. Only after we have won a series of victories does the conflict become more tolerable.

Today Satan is patrolling the earth seeking recruits to bring into his kingdom. He has brought in the New Age based on the Old Age lies of Babylon. Those who do not fall in line with his program are targeted for extinction. But in the end his schemes will fail.

In that great day of conflict God's people will overcome him on the same basis that we can overcome him today.

"And they overcame him because of the blood of the Lamb and because of the word of their testimony, and they did not love their life even to death" (Revelation 12:11).

Thankfully, the blood of the Lamb has not lost its power.

NOTES

Chapter 1

1. Marilyn Ferguson, *The Aquarian Conspiracy* (Los Angeles: Jeremy P. Tarcher, 1980), p. 23.
2. Andrew Greeley, *American Health*, Jan./Feb. 1987, p. 47.
3. Texe Marrs, *Dark Secrets of the New Age* (Westchester, Ill.: Crossway Books, 1987), p. 26.

Chapter 2

1. *Time*, May 16, 1988, p. 25.
2. *Training*, Sept. 1987, p. 26.
3. Napoleon Hill, *Grow Rich with Peace of Mind* (New York: Ballantine Books, 1967), pp. 158–60.
4. *Fortune*, Nov. 23, 1987, p. 95.
5. *Ibid.*, p. 96.
6. *Ibid.*
7. *Ibid.*
8. Robert A. Morey, *Reincarnation and Christianity*

(Minneapolis: Bethany Fellowship, 1980), p. 28.

9. *Time*, Dec. 7, 1987, p. 64.

10. Whitley Strieber, *Communion* (New York: Beech Tree Books, William Morrow, 1987), p. 215.

11. Maharishi, *Science of Being and Art of Living* (Bergenfield, N.J.: New American Library, 1963), pp. 299–300. Quoted by Pat Means in *The Mystical Maze* (Campus Crusade for Christ, 1976), p. 135.

12. *New Thought*, Fall 1983, p. 5.

13. Allan Bloom, *The Closing of the American Mind* (New York: Simon and Schuster, 1987), p. 27.

14. *Kindred Spirit*, Summer 1987, p. 5.

15. Terry Cole-Whittaker, *The Inner Path from Where You Are to Where You Want to Be* (New York: Fawcett Crest, 1986), p. 81.

Chapter 3

1. *Chicago Tribune*, Aug. 15, 1985.

2. *Ibid.*

3. *Ibid.*

4. Marilyn Ferguson, *op. cit.*, p. 23.

5. *Ibid.*, p. 24.

6. Shirley MacLaine, *Out on a Limb* (New York: Bantam Books, 1983).

7. Shirley MacLaine, *Dancing in the Light* (New York: Bantam Books, 1985).

8. *Money*, Sept. 1987, p. 169.

9. Napoleon Hill, *Think and Grow Rich* (New York: Fawcett Crest, 1979).

10. *Defending the Faith*, vol. 3 (Chattanooga: The John Ankerberg Show, 1986), p. 156. This is a written transcript of television programs aired on the John Ankerberg Show in 1986.

11. Terry Cole-Whittaker, *op. cit.*, p. 75.

12. *What's So?* (magazine of the *est* organization), January 1975.

13. *Man, Myth, and Magic*, vol. 3 (New York: Marshall

Cavendish, 1970), p. 436.

14. Karen Hoyt and J. Isamu Yamamoto, eds. *The New Age Rage* (Old Tappan, N.J.: Fleming H. Revell, 1987). This book contains excellent chapters by various authors on different aspects of the New Age Movement.

15. *Ibid.*, p. 23.

Chapter 4

1. *Chicago Tribune*, Oct. 23, 1987.

2. Fritjof Capra, *The Tao of Physics* (Boston: Shambhala, 1975), p. 11.

3. *Time*, May 23, 1983, p. 22.

4. *AFA Journal*, July 1988, p. 22.

5. Shirley MacLaine, *Out on a Limb*, p. 107.

6. Allan Watts, *Beat Zen, Square Zen, and Zen* (San Francisco: City Lights, 1959), p. 10.

7. Terry Cole-Whittaker, *op. cit.*, p. 39.

8. *National Geographic*, July 1977, p. 63.

9. *Farm Journal*, Mid-March 1986, p. 19.

10. Mike Samuels and Hal Z. Bennett, *Well Body, Well Earth—Sierra Club Environmental Health Sourcebook* (San Francisco: Sierra Club Books, 1983), p. 69.

Chapter 5

1. *Dallas Times Herald*, June 19, 1968.

2. Richard Grenier, *The Ghandi Nobody Knows* (Nashville: Thomas Nelson, 1983), p. 71.

3. Shirley MacLaine, *Out on a Limb*, p. 199.

4. F. LaGard Smith, *Out on a Broken Limb* (Eugene, Ore.: Harvest House, 1986), p. 188.

5. John Snyder, *Reincarnation vs. Resurrection* (Chicago: Moody Press, 1984), pp. 27–30.

6. F. LaGard Smith, *op. cit.*, p. 166–67.

Chapter 6

1. *SPC Journal*, 1982, p. 1.

2. *Sannayas*, no. 5, Sept./Oct. 1978, p. 34. Quoted by John

Ankerberg and John Weldon, *The Facts on the New Age Movement* (Chattanooga: The John Ankerberg Evangelistic Association, 1988), p. 10.

3. Rajneesh in Swami Anand Yarti, *The Sound of Running Water: A Photobiography of Bhagwan Shree Rajneesh and His Work*, 1974–1978 (Poona, India: Poona Rajneesh Foundation, 1980), p. 382. Quoted by John Ankerberg and John Weldon, *op. cit.*, p. 22.

4. Vivekananda in Swami Nikhilananda (compiler) *Vivekananda the Yoga and Other Works* (New York: Ramabrishma Vivekananada Center, 1953), p. 530. Quoted by John Ankerberg and John Weldon, *op. cit.*, p. 22.

5. Os Guinness, *The Dust of Death* (Downers Grove, Ill.: InterVarsity Press, 1973), p. 221.

6. Dave Hunt and T.A. McMahon, *America—The Sorcerer's New Apprentice* (Eugene, Ore.: Harvest House, 1988), p. 223.

7. *Radix*, Nov./Dec. 1979.

8. *SPC Newsletter*, 1982, p. 2.

9. *Ibid.*

10. Terry Cole-Whittaker, *op. cit.*, p. 119.

11. Richard Grenier, *op. cit.*, p. 79.

12. Information on these commandments may be obtained from: Box 110, Elberton, Georgia 30635.

13. Moira Timms, *Prophecies and Predictions: Everyone's Guide to the Coming Changes*, pp. 57–8. Quoted by Texe Marrs, *op. cit.*, p. 144.

Chapter 7

1. Alice Bailey, *Problems of Humanity* (New York: Luci Publishing Co., 1945), p. 166. This invocation has been translated into more than 40 languages and is therefore familiar to millions around the world.

2. Andrew Greeley, *op. cit.*, p. 48.

3. Marilyn Ferguson, *op. cit.*, p. 89.

4. C.S. Lewis, *The Screwtape Letters* (New York: Macmillan Co., 1943), p. 39.

5. Marilyn Ferguson, *op. cit.*, p. 24.

6. *Ibid.*, p. 85.

7. S.N. Dasgupta, *Hindu Mysticism* (New York: Frederick Unger Co., 1927), p. 76.

8. *Ibid.*, p. 79.

9. *Ibid.*, p. 80.

10. *Ibid.*

11. Annette Hollander, *How to Help Your Child Have a Spiritual Life* (New York: A&W Publishers, 1980), p. 31.

12. *National Enquirer*, Nov. 1987, p. 3.

13. John Ankerberg and John Weldon, *The Facts on Channeling* (Chattanooga: The John Ankerberg Evangelistic Association, 1988), p. 8.

14. These are observations drawn from our personal counseling and reading of the experiences of those who have become involved in occult phenomena.

Chapter 8

1. *Venture Inward*, Sept./Oct. 1987, p. 45.

2. *Ibid.*, p. 46.

3. *Ibid.*, p. 47.

4. Paul Vitz, *Psychology as Religion: The Cult of Self Worship* (Grand Rapids: Eerdmans, 1977), p. 10.

5. Carl Jung, *Answers to Job* (London: Routledge and Paul, 1954).

6. Eric Fromm, *You Shall Be As Gods* (New York: Holt, Rinehart, and Winston, 1966).

7. William Kilpatrick, *Psychological Seduction* (Nashville: Thomas Nelson, 1983), p. 43.

8. Robert Schuller, *Self-Esteem—The New Reformation* (Waco, Texas: Word Books, 1982), pp. 26–7.

9. *Ibid.*, p. 14.

10. *Ibid.*, p. 127.

11. Robert Schuller, *Peace of Mind Through Possibility Thinking* (Old Tappan, N.J.: Fleming H. Revell, 1977), pp. 131–32.

12. C.S. Lewis, *op. cit.*, pp. 52, 126.

13. Claude Bristol, *The Magic of Believing* (Hollywood, Calif.: Wilshire Book Co., 1966), p. 37.

14. *Fundamentalist Journal*, Nov. 1987, p. 15.

15. Francis MacNutt, *Healing* (New York: Bantam Books, 1974), p. 170.

Chapter 9

1. Phil Phillips, *Turmoil in the Toybox* (Lancaster, Pa.: Starburst Publishers, 1986), p. 37.

2. *Chicago Tribune*, January 27, 1985.

3. *Ibid.*

4. *Ibid.*

5. Phil Phillips, *op. cit.*, p. 116.

6. Frances Adeney, "Educators Look East," *SCP Journal*, Winter 1981–82, p. 28.

7. *Ibid.*, p. 29.

8. *Ibid.*

9. John Ankerberg, *Defending the Faith*, p. 150.

10. *Newsweek*, May 13, 1985, p. 68.

11. Michael Haynes, *The God of Rock* (Lindale, Texas: Priority Publications, 1982), p. 35.

12. *Ibid.*, p. 53.

13. *Ibid.*, p. 157.

14. *Ibid.*

15. *Ibid.*, p. 198.

16. *Ibid.*

Chapter 10

1. Gerald Suster, *Hitler: The Occult Messiah* (New York: St. Martin Press, 1981), p. 120. Quoted by Dave Hunt, *Peace, Prosperity, and the Coming Holocaust* (Eugene, Ore.: Harvest House, 1983), p. 137.

2. Alice Bailey, *The Externalization of the Hierarchy* (New York: Lucis Publishing Co., n.d.), pp. 453–54.

3. "H.G. Wells, A Forerunner," *The Beacon*, May/June 1977. Quoted by Constance Cumbey, *The Hidden Dangers of the Rainbow* (Lafayette, La.: Huntington House, 1983), p. 125.

Footnotes

4. Marilyn Ferguson, *op. cit.*, p. 23.

5. Benjamin Creme, *The Reappearance of Christ and Masters of Wisdom* (London: Tara Press, 1979), p. 81.

6. *The Economist*, Jan. 1988, p. 9.

7. Alice Bailey, *op. cit.*, pp. 453–54.

8. Brigham Young, *Deseret News*, June 18, 1873, p. 308. Quoted by Ed Decker and Dave Hunt, *The God Makers* (Eugene, Ore.: Harvest House, 1984), p. 30.

9. William Bowen, Jr., *Globalism: America's Demise* (Lafayette, La.: Huntington House, 1984), p. 131.

10. Alice Bailey, *op. cit.*, p. 191.

11. Barry Goldwater, *With No Apologies* (New York: William Morrow, 1979), p. 280.

12. Dave Hunt, *Peace, Prosperity, and the Coming Holocaust*, p. 10.

Chapter 11

1. George G. Hunter III, *The Contagious Congregation: Frontiers in Evangelism and Church Growth* (New York: Abingdon Press, 1975), p. 79.

2. John Piper, *Desiring God—Meditations of a Christian Hedonist* (Portland, Ore.: Multnomah Press, 1986), p. 19.

3. *Ibid.*, p. 203.